# Fecal-Indicator Bacteria Concentrations in the Illinois River between Hennepin and Peoria, Illinois: 2007–08

By David H. Dupré, Jon E. Hortness, Paul J. Terrio, and Jennifer B. Sharpe

Prepared in cooperation with the Tri-County Regional Planning Commission

Open File Report 2012–1075

**U.S. Department of the Interior**
**U.S. Geological Survey**

**U.S. Department of the Interior**
KEN SALAZAR, Secretary

**U.S. Geological Survey**
Marcia K. McNutt, Director

U.S. Geological Survey, Reston, Virginia: 2012

For more information on the USGS—the Federal source for science about the Earth, its natural and living resources, natural hazards, and the environment, visit http://www.usgs.gov or call 1–888–ASK–USGS.

For an overview of USGS information products, including maps, imagery, and publications, visit http://www.usgs.gov/pubprod

To order this and other USGS information products, visit http://store.usgs.gov

Suggested citation:
Dupré, D.H., Hortness, J.E., Terrio, P.J., and Sharpe, J.B., 2012, Fecal-indicator bacteria concentrations in the Illinois River between Hennepin and Peoria, Illinois: 2007–08: U.S. Geological Survey Open-File Report 2012–1075, 32 p.

# Contents

# Figures

# Tables

# Conversion Factors, Vertical Datum, and Abbreviations

Inch/Pound to SI

| Multiply | By | To obtain |
|---|---|---|
| Length | | |
| inch (in.) | 2.54 | centimeter (cm) |
| inch (in.) | 25.4 | millimeter (mm) |
| foot (ft) | 0.3048 | meter (m) |
| mile (mi) | 1.609 | kilometer (km) |
| Area | | |
| square mile (mi$^2$) | 259.0 | hectare (ha) |
| square mile (mi$^2$) | 2.590 | square kilometer (km$^2$) |
| Flow rate | | |
| cubic foot per second (ft$^3$/s) | 0.02832 | cubic meter per second (m$^3$/s) |

Temperature in degrees Celsius (°C) may be converted to degrees Fahrenheit (°F) as follows:

°F=(1.8×°C)+32

Vertical coordinate information is referenced to North American Vertical Datum of 1988 (NAVD 88).

Horizontal coordinate information is referenced to North American Datum of 1983 (NAD 83).

Altitude, as used in this report, refers to distance above the vertical datum.

Specific conductance is given in microsiemens per centimeter at 25 degrees Celsius (µS/cm at 25 °C).

Concentrations of chemical constituents in water are given either in milligrams per liter (mg/L) or micrograms per liter (µg/L).

Bacteria concentrations are given in colony-forming units per 100 milliliters (CFU/100 mL).

Water year is the 12-month period October 1 for any given year through September 30 of the following year. The water year is designated by the calendar year in which it ends and which includes 9 of the 12 months.

# Abbreviations

| | |
|---|---|
| CSO | combined sewer overflow |
| E. coli | Escherichia coli |
| FC | fecal coliform |
| FIB | fecal-indicator bacteria |
| IEPA | Illinois Environmental Protection Agency |
| TMDL | Total Maximum Daily Load |
| USEPA | U.S. Environmental Protection Agency |
| USGS | U.S. Geological Survey |

# Fecal-Indicator Bacteria Concentrations in the Illinois River between Hennepin and Peoria, Illinois: 2007–08

By David H. Dupré, Jon E. Hortness, Paul J. Terrio, and Jennifer B. Sharpe

## Abstract

The Illinois Environmental Protection Agency has designated portions of the Illinois River in Peoria, Woodford, and Tazewell Counties, Illinois, as impaired owing to the presence of fecal coliform bacteria. The U.S. Geological Survey, in cooperation with the Tri-County Regional Planning Commission, examined the water quality in the Illinois River and major tributaries within a 47-mile reach between Peoria and Hennepin, Ill., during water year 2008 (October 2007–September 2008). Investigations included synoptic (snapshot) sampling at multiple locations in a 1-day period: once in October 2007 during lower streamflow conditions, and again in June 2008 during higher streamflow conditions. Five locations in the study area were monitored for the entire year at monthly or more frequent intervals. Two indicator bacteria were analyzed in each water sample: fecal coliform and *Escherichia coli* (*E. coli*). Streamflow information from previously established monitoring locations in the study area was used in the analysis. Correlation analyses were used to characterize the relation between the two fecal-indicator bacteria and the relation of either indicator to streamflow. Concentrations of the two measured fecal-indicator bacteria correlated well for all samples analyzed (r = 0.94, p <0.001), indicating a strong linear correlation. Presence of one fecal-indicator bacteria generally indicates the presence of another at a similar magnitude and may support substitution of generalized data gaps for other analyses. Hydrologic conditions during the study period can be characterized as wetter than normal, with the mean annual flow in the Illinois River about 37-percent above the long-term average. However, for the Illinois River below Peoria Lake at Peoria, a statistically significant negative correlation coefficient indicates a weak inverse relation between values of streamflow and fecal-indicator bacteria (fecal coliform: rho = −0.44, p = 0.0129; *E. coli*: rho = −0.43, p = 0.0157). The correlation between fecal indicators and streamflow in tributaries or in the Illinois River at Hennepin was found to be statistically significant, yet moderate in strength with coefficient values ranging from r = 0.4 to 0.6. Indirect observations from the June 2008 higher flow synoptic event may indicate continued effects from combined storm and sanitary sewers in the vicinity of the Illinois River near Peoria, Ill., contributing to observed single-sample exceedance of the State criterion for fecal coliform.

## Introduction

Portions of the Illinois River in Peoria, Woodford, and Tazewell Counties, Illinois, are designated as impaired by the Illinois Environmental Protection Agency (IEPA) owing to the presence of fecal coliform (FC) bacteria (Illinois Environmental Protection Agency, 2008). FC bacteria are used as an indicator of possible pathogens. Elevated concentrations of FC bacteria could cause a violation of the State water-quality standard for general-use waters primarily because of potential ingestion or physical exposure. Epidemiological research has demonstrated a relation between illness rates and the proximity to known FC bacteria point sources (Cabelli and others, 1982; Wade and others, 2006). Combined sewer overflows (CSOs) from the City of Peoria occur periodically as a result of moderate to heavy rainfall in the area (City of Peoria, 2010). CSOs result in the release of storm water, along with raw sewage, to the Illinois River, which causes elevated bacteria concentrations in the vicinity of the outfalls. However, FC bacteria data collected in the Illinois River upstream of the City of Peoria CSO discharge points indicate the Illinois River often has background concentrations of FC bacteria that exceed the water-quality standard for general-use waters. Both point sources and diffuse sources of FC bacteria may contribute to the exceedances of the water-quality standard upstream of Peoria (Sercu and others, 2009).

The Tri-County Regional Planning Commission proposed to conduct a study to better identify the likely source areas of the bacterial contamination in the river upstream from Peoria. The overall study objectives were to evaluate the impacts that point sources and diffuse sources have on the concentrations of FC bacteria in the Illinois River between Hennepin, Ill., and the outlet of Peoria Lake at Peoria, Ill. As part of this study, the U.S. Geological Survey (USGS) evaluated bacteria concentrations in streams tributary to the Illinois River between Hennepin and Peoria, Ill., and investigated the possibility that some of these streams may be sources of elevated bacteria concentrations in the Illinois River.

After this study began, the U.S. Environmental Protection Agency (USEPA) and IEPA initiated the development of a total maximum daily load (TMDL) for FC bacteria in this reach of the Illinois River. The bacteria data collected by the USGS will be a significant resource in the development of these TMDLs. The development of a TMDL for FC bacteria assumes the bacteria, and any associated pathogens, result from direct human-controlled activities (either from point sources or diffuse sources) and that successful compliance with a water-quality standard can be achieved through managing or removing the sources of bacteria. Several limitations to this assumption for FC bacteria should be noted:

- they are not specific to human sources,

- they can persist in a more-varied manner than the associated pathogens they are meant to indicate (Anderson and others, 2005; Wade and others, 2006), and

- they can become non-culturable (Leadbetter, 1997; Statham and McMeekin, 1994).

Generally, *Escherichia coli (E. coli)* are thought to be a more accurate indicator of potential human or animal-influenced pathogenic organisms than FC bacteria because they are a subset of the FC bacteria and reside in the gut of warm-blooded creatures (U.S. Food and Drug Administration, 1998). Other FCs are not necessarily unique to warm-blooded animals.

## Purpose and Scope

This report describes the results of sampling for FC and *E. coli* bacteria (collectively referred to as fecal-indicator bacteria (FIB)) along the main stem and various tributaries of the Illinois River within the study area during water year 2008. Simple linear regressions of the two FIB data types were performed against each other and against streamflow. The hydrologic conditions of the study period are compared against long-term records to describe the observed FIB concentrations in relation to historical streamflows.

## Description of Study Area

The general area for this study includes the main stem of the Illinois River from Hennepin downstream to Peoria, in addition to several small basins that are tributary to this reach of the Illinois River (fig. 1). The main stem reach within the study area extends approximately 47 river miles and receives inflows from about 1,500 mi² of contributing drainage area. Major tributaries to the study reach include Big Bureau Creek (491 mi²), Senachwine Creek (87 mi²), and Farm Creek (61

mi²). The study area also encompasses several in-channel and off-channel lakes including Senachwine Lake, Upper Peoria Lake, and Peoria Lake.

The drainage areas along the study reach generally are rural with the exception of the area in and around Peoria, which is mostly urban. Land use varies throughout the region with row-crop farming being the most common, followed by deciduous forest areas and pasture lands (fig. 2).

Combined sanitary and storm sewers are present in Peoria and CSOs are common during higher intensity rainfall events. CSO occurrences average about 28 times per year, generally when total rainfall amounts exceed about 0.15 in. for any storm event. There are 20 potential overflow points located in Peoria (City of Peoria, 2010). Several smaller towns located along the Illinois River and within the various contributing drainage basins discharge effluent from wastewater-treatment plants to the main stem or tributaries (fig. 1).

## Previous Investigations

Several investigations regarding the presence of bacteria in the Illinois River were previously conducted. Greenfield (1924) studied bacteria concentrations in the approximately 80-mi reach from LaSalle to Kingston Mines. Hoskins and others (1927) studied the entire length of the Illinois River from its origin near Joliet, Ill., downstream to the confluence with the Mississippi River near Grafton, Ill. (approximately 275 mi).

Lin and Evans (1980) analyzed water samples collected from the Illinois River at Peoria on a weekly basis during June 1971–May 1976. They found that bacteria concentrations ranged widely throughout the year, with the highest concentrations generally occurring during the winter and summer months. Building upon the work by Lin and Evans (1980), Lin and Beuscher (1994) analyzed weekly water samples during June 1976–May 1986. They found that throughout the 15-year period (1971–86) only about 17 percent of the samples were in compliance with the existing water-quality standard (geometric mean of 200 colony-forming units per 100 mL CFU/100 mL), from a minimum of five samples collected in a 30-day period; or 400 CFU/100 mL in a single sample).

The IEPA has in the past and continues to collect and analyze water samples at various locations within the study area as part of their Ambient Water Quality Monitoring Network. The samples are collected approximately every 6 weeks and are analyzed for over 55 parameters including FC bacteria.

## Hydrologic Perspective

The period of data collection for this study, in general, coincided with a period of relatively high precipitation across much of central and northern Illinois, including most of the

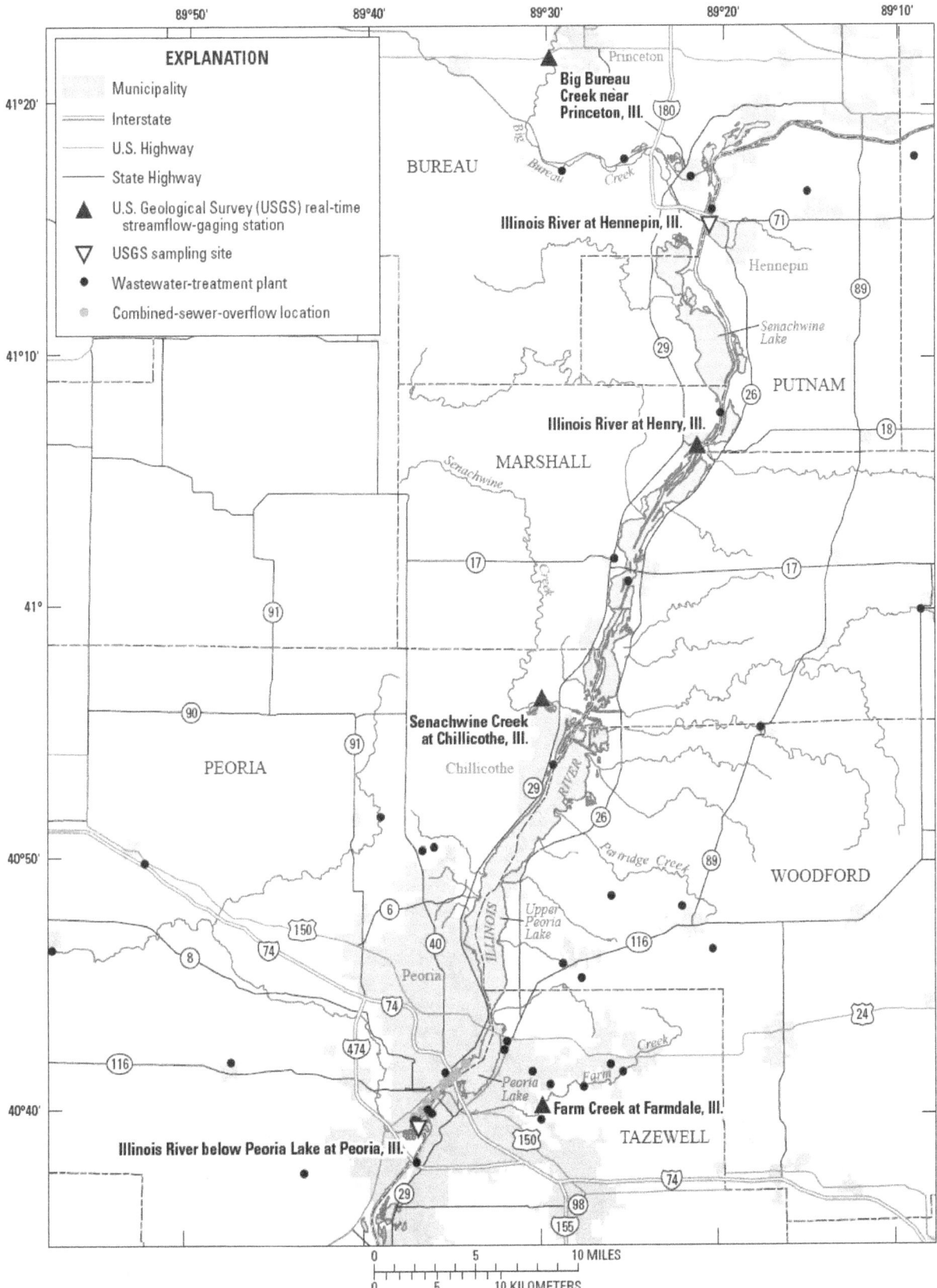

**Figure 1.** General study area, locations of combined-sewer-overflow points, and wastewater-treatment plant discharge points between Hennepin and Peoria, Illinois.

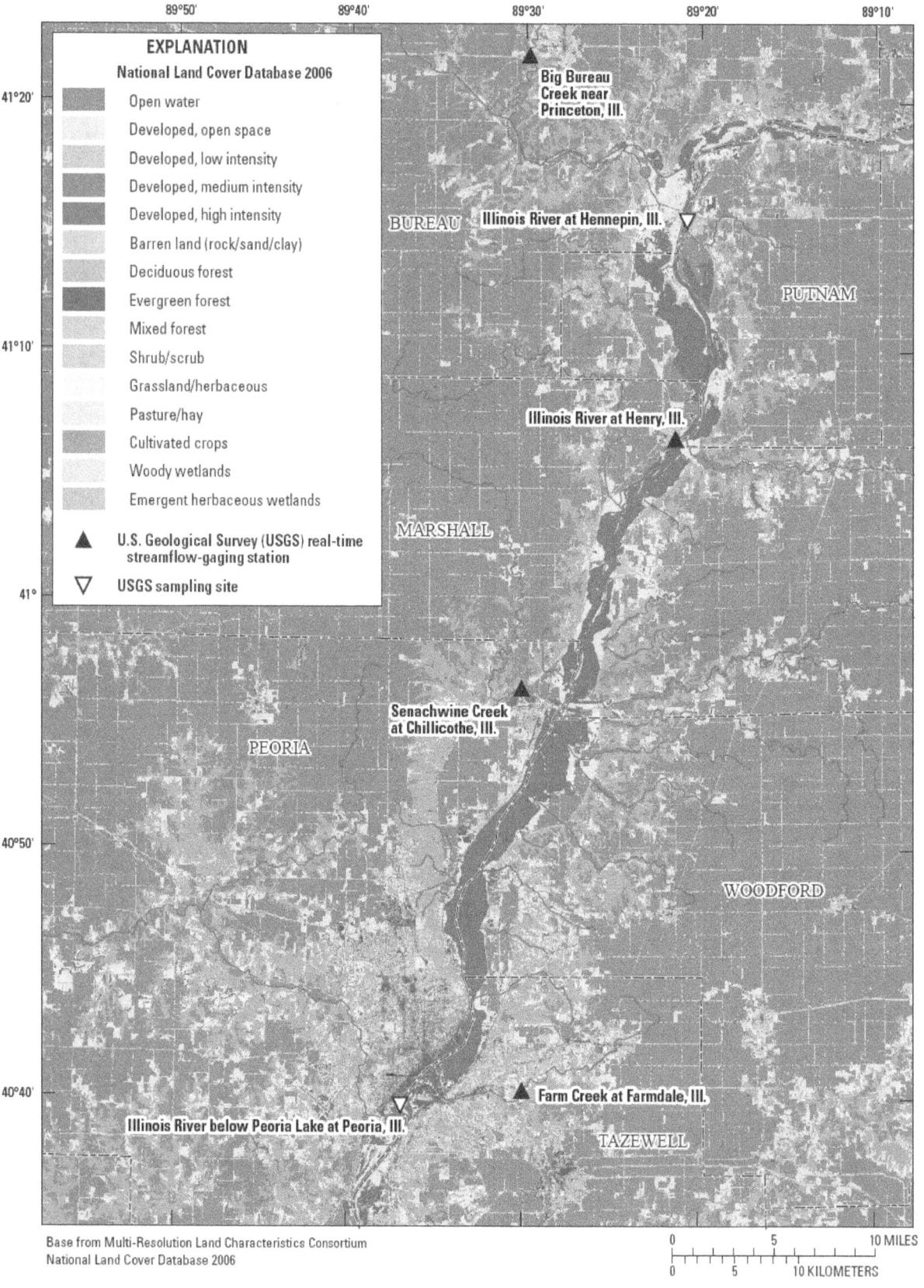

**Figure 2.** Land cover in the general study area between Hennepin and Peoria, Illinois.

Illinois River Basin. Average precipitation levels across the State for October–December 2007 were near normal to just slightly below normal (30-year average; 1971–2000). However, January–June 2008 was the wettest first 6 months of the year on record (since 1895), with a statewide average of 27.7 in., which was 8.3 in. above normal. The statewide average precipitation for the entire year (2008) was 50.7 in.—11.4 in. above normal—resulting in the second wettest year on record (Illinois State Water Survey, 2010). Specific locations within the Illinois River Basin showed similar precipitation results:

Chicago O'Hare International Airport: October–December 2007, 1.7 in. below normal; 2008, 14.6 in. above normal

Ottawa, Ill.: October–December 2007, 2.4 in. below normal; 2008, 6.6 in. above normal

Peoria Regional Airport: October–December 2007, 0.8 in. below normal; 2008, 10.5 in. above normal (National Oceanic and Atmospheric Administration, 2007, 2008).

As a result of the above-normal precipitation, streamflows in the Illinois River and in the tributaries within the study area were well above the long-term average. The annual mean streamflow for the Illinois River at Henry, Ill., (USGS streamflow-gaging station number 05558300, which is located north-central in the study area), was 20,600 ft³/s for water year 2008. This was about 37-percent higher than the long-term (1982–2008) annual mean streamflow of 15,000 ft³/s. Similarly, the annual mean streamflow for Big Bureau Creek at Princeton, Ill., (USGS streamflow-gaging station number 05556500, a tributary to the Illinois River near the upstream end of the study area), was 282 ft³/s for water year 2008. This was about 97-percent higher than the long-term (1936–2008) annual mean streamflow of 143 ft³/s. Hydrographs showing comparisons between water year 2008 and long-term daily mean streamflows for the Illinois River at Henry and Big Bureau Creek at Princeton are presented in figures 3 and 4, respectively.

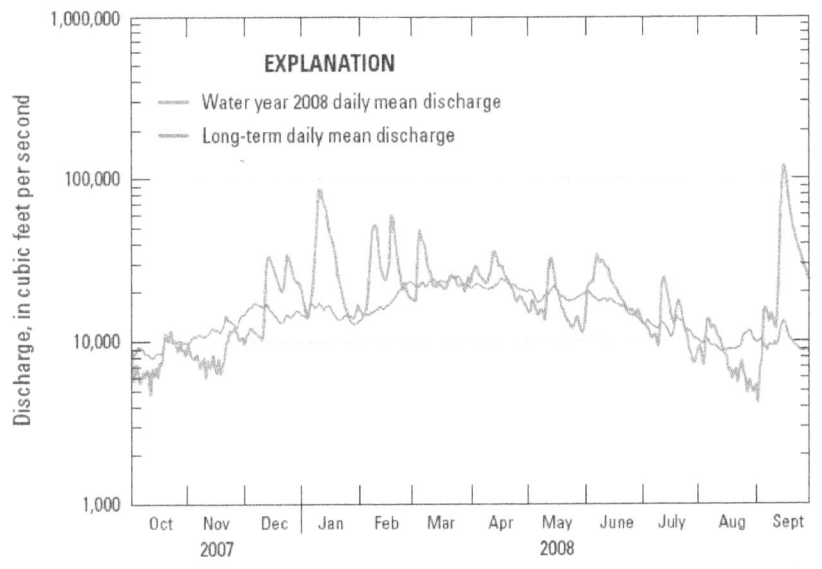

**Figure 3.** Comparison between water year 2008 and long-term daily mean streamflows for the Illinois River at Henry, Illinois (U.S. Geological Survey streamflow-gaging station number 05558300).

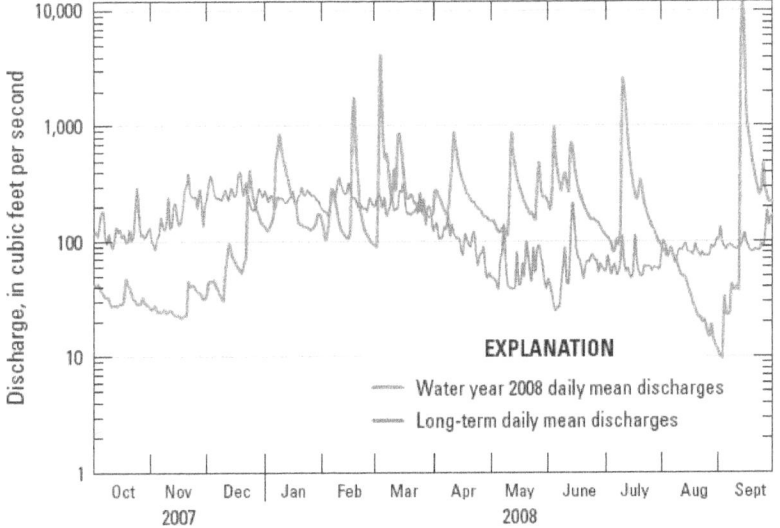

**Figure 4.** Comparison between water year 2008 and long-term daily mean streamflows for Big Bureau Creek at Princeton, Illinois (U.S. Geological Survey streamflow-gaging station number 05556500).

# Data Collection

Samples were collected from the main stem of the Illinois River at Hennepin and Peoria, Ill., and near the outlets of three major tributaries to the Illinois River (Big Bureau Creek, Senachwine Creek, and Farm Creek) during the same time period. In addition, four sets of samples were collected at two locations in the upper portion of the Partridge Creek Watershed.

Two intensive synoptic sampling efforts also were completed under different environmental conditions. During these efforts, samples were collected at multiple locations along the main stem of the Illinois River and in several tributaries within the study area (fig. 5).

Two types of FIB were assessed: FC and *Escherichia coli* (*E. coli*). All samples were collected and processed following USGS standard protocols and methods documented in the USGS National Field Manual (U.S. Geological Survey, variously dated); specific details on FIB sampling are found in chapter A7 (Myers and others, 2007).

## Periodic Sampling

Samples were collected approximately weekly at the Illinois River at Hennepin, Ill. (USGS streamflow-gaging station number 05556200) (table 1), and at the Illinois River below Peoria Lake at Peoria, Ill. (USGS streamflow-gaging station number 05562200) (table 2), for a total of 31 times during water year 2008. All of the samples were analyzed for both FC and *E. coli*. In addition, the following water-quality parameters were measured on-site during the sample collection: air temperature, water temperature, barometric pressure, dissolved oxygen, pH, and specific conductance. Streamflow is estimated at sites without continuous monitoring.

Samples were collected on a monthly basis near the outlets of three major tributaries to the Illinois River within the study area. A total of 11 samples were collected at Big Bureau Creek near Princeton, Ill. (USGS streamflow-gaging station number 05556500) (table 3); a total of 10 samples were collected at Farm Creek at Farmdale, Ill. (USGS streamflow-gaging station number 05560500) (table 4); and a total of 9 samples were collected at Senachwine Creek at Chillicothe, Ill. (USGS streamflow-gaging station number 05559700) (table 5).

Finally, four sets of samples (table 6) were collected at two locations in the upper portion of the Partridge Creek Watershed in an attempt to identify potential sources of bacteria within a specified stream reach. Again, all samples were analyzed for both FC and *E. coli*, and observations of air temperature, water temperature, barometric pressure, dissolved oxygen, pH, and specific conductance were measured on-site during sampling.

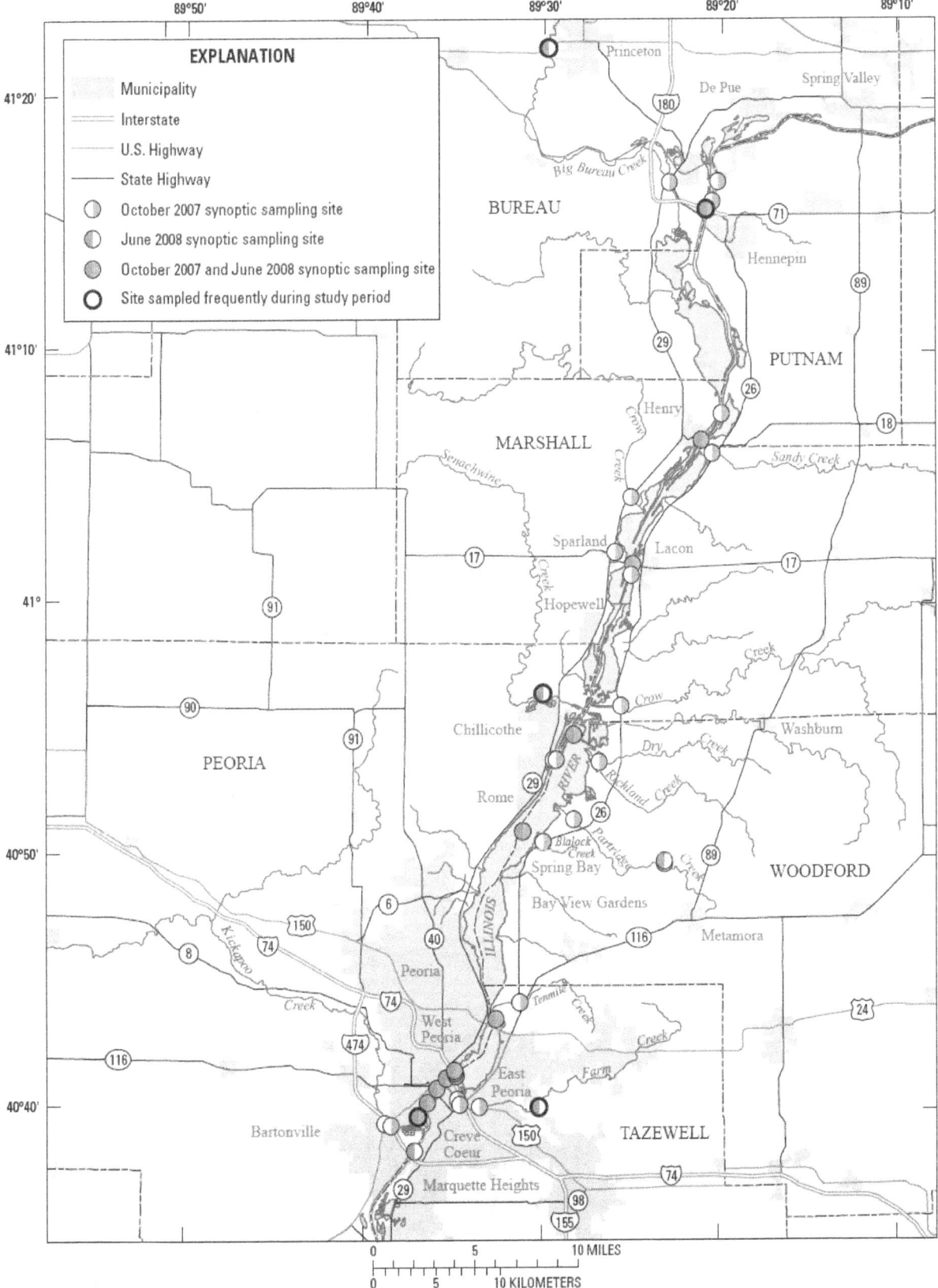

**Figure 5.** Locations sampled during October 2007 and June 2008 synoptic samplings and frequently during the study period between Princeton and Peoria, Illinois.

**Table 1.**  Physical, chemical, and bacterial data for the Illinois River at Hennepin, Illinois (U.S. Geological Survey streamflow-gaging station number 05556200), during water year 2008 (October 2007–September 2008)

[hhmm, hour minute; Hg, mercury; MF, membrane filter; col/100 mL, colonies per 100 milliliters; ft, foot; ft³/s, cubic foot per second; micron, micrometer; mg/L, milligrams per liter; mm, millimeter; C, degrees Celsius; µS/cm, microsiemens per centimeter; —, no data; E, estimated; k, counts outside acceptable range; CDT, central daylight time; CST, central standard time]

| Sample notes | Date | Time (24-hour clock, hhmm) | Barometric pressure, (mm Hg) (00025) | Temperature, air, (°C) (00020) | Discharge, (ft³/s) (00060) | Dissolved oxygen, water, unfiltered, (mg/L) (00300) | pH, water, unfiltered, field, (standard units) (00400) | Specific conductance, water, unfiltered, (µS/cm at 25 °C) (00095) | Temperature, water, (°C) (00010) | Gage height, (ft) (00065) | Number of sampling points, (count) (00063) | Escherichia coli, modified m-TEC MF method, water (col/100 mL) (90902) | Fecal coliform, M-FC MF (0.45 micron) method, water, (col/100 mL) (31616) |
|---|---|---|---|---|---|---|---|---|---|---|---|---|---|
| Median values from synoptic cross-section | Oct 10 2007 | 1442 CDT | 748 | E12.0 | E6350 | 9.3 | 8.5 | 850 | 21.8 | — | 4 | E14.5 k | E28 k |
| Cross-section part 1 of 2; mid-channel | Oct 18 2007 | 1410 CST | 725 | — | E8560 | 9.4 | 8.2 | 860 | 18.5 | — | 1 | 140 | 93 |
| Cross-section part 2 of 2; left-channel | Oct 18 2007 | 1445 CST | 725 | — | E8560 | 9.4 | 8.3 | 872 | 18.5 | — | 1 | 81 | 170 |
| Mid-channel grab | Oct 25 2007 | 1100 CST | 754 | 7.2 | E9340 | 9.4 | 8.2 | 863 | 14.9 | — | 1 | 48 | 50 |
| Mid-channel grab | Nov 1 2007 | 1145 CST | 757 | 10.0 | E8790 | 10.9 | 8.3 | 831 | 12.9 | — | 1 | 48 | 89 |
| Mid-channel grab | Nov 7 2007 | 0930 CST | 756 | -3.8 | E6820 | 13.2 | 8.8 | 816 | 9.6 | — | 1 | E17 k | 60 |
| Cross-section composite | Nov 15 2007 | 0855 CST | 750 | 1.7 | E6900 | 12.2 | 8.2 | 856 | 9.4 | — | 3 | 76 | 38 |
| Cross-section composite | Nov 21 2007 | 0850 CST | 745 | — | E9460 | 13.2 | 8.8 | 888 | 9.5 | — | 3 | 38 | 51 |
| Cross-section composite | Nov 28 2007 | 1135 CST | 746 | 4.4 | E10300 | 12.7 | 8.4 | 833 | 5.0 | — | 3 | 110 | E44 k |
| Cross-section composite | Dec 5 2007 | 1045 CST | 747 | -1.1 | E12100 | 14.3 | 8.5 | 792 | 1.7 | — | 3 | 140 | E54 k |
| Cross-section composite | Dec 12 2007 | 1025 CST | 756 | -1.1 | E17000 | 13.5 | 8.3 | 984 | 2.2 | — | 3 | 550 | 300 |
| Cross-section composite | Dec 19 2007 | 1010 CST | 750 | -5.0 | E23700 | 13.9 | 8.0 | 976 | 1.6 | — | 3 | 170 | 130 |
| Cross-section composite | Jan 3 2008 | 0955 CST | 763 | -15.0 | E15400 | 14.7 | 8.3 | 1010 | 0.0 | — | 3 | 73 | 48 |
| Cross-section composite | Jan 9 2008 | 1105 CST | 751 | 2.0 | E51800 | 10.5 | 7.9 | 882 | 7.9 | — | 3 | 1600 | 670 |
| Cross-section composite | Jan 16 2008 | 0945 CST | 748 | 0.2 | E46200 | 12.8 | 7.9 | 564 | 2.4 | — | 3 | 230 | E200 k |
| Mid-channel grab, iced conditions | Jan 24 2008 | 0945 CST | 758 | -20.0 | E16400 | 13.2 | 8.0 | 790 | 0.1 | — | 1 | 110 | 150 |
| Cross-section composite | Feb 6 2008 | 1000 CST | 729 | 0.0 | E24300 | 13.3 | 8.0 | 1090 | 1.6 | — | 3 | E450 k | E330 k |
| Cross-section composite | Mar 12 2008 | 1235 CST | — | 3.9 | E21900 | 12.8 | 8.1 | 901 | 3.3 | — | 3 | 120 | 73 |
| Cross-section composite | Mar 26 2008 | 1015 CST | 752 | 5.2 | E22300 | 12.0 | 8.1 | 819 | 6.8 | — | 3 | 110 | E55 k |
| Cross-section composite | Apr 2 2008 | 0940 CST | 759 | 5.7 | E27500 | 12.0 | 8.1 | 977 | 8.2 | — | 3 | 200 | 130 |
| Cross-section composite | Apr 9 2008 | 1050 CST | 752 | 5.7 | E22700 | 11.1 | 8.1 | 874 | 11.0 | — | 3 | 150 | 120 |

**Table 1.**  Physical, chemical, and bacterial data for the Illinois River at Hennepin, Illinois (U.S. Geological Survey streamflow-gaging station number 05556200), during water year 2008 (October 2007–September 2008).—Continued

[hhmm, hour minute; Hg, mercury; MF, membrane filter; col/100 mL, colonies per 100 milliliters; ft, foot; ft³/s, cubic foot per second; micron, micrometer; mg/L, milligrams per liter; mm, millimeter; C, degrees Celsius; µS/cm, microsiemens per centimeter; —, no data; E, estimated; k, counts outside acceptable range; CDT, central daylight time; CST, central standard time]

| Sample notes | Date | Time (24-hour clock, hhmm) | Barometric pressure (mm Hg) | Temperature, air, (°C) | Discharge, (ft³/s) | Dissolved oxygen, water, unfiltered, (mg/L) | pH, water, unfiltered, field, (standard units) | Specific conductance, water, unfiltered, (µS/cm at 25 °C) | Temperature, water, (°C) | Gage height, (ft) | Number of sampling points, (count) | *Escherichia coli*, modified m-TEC MF method, water, (col/100 mL) | Fecal coliform, M-FC MF (0.45 micron) method, water, (col/100 mL) |
|---|---|---|---|---|---|---|---|---|---|---|---|---|---|
| | | | (00025) | (00020) | (00060) | (00300) | (00400) | (00095) | (00010) | (00065) | (00063) | (90902) | (31616) |
| Cross-section composite | Apr 16 2008 | 0955 CST | 745 | 10.9 | E28600 | 11.3 | 8.1 | 838 | 10.0 | — | 3 | 150 | E54 k |
| Cross-section composite | Apr 23 2008 | 0940 CST | 754 | 17.1 | E20400 | 10.2 | 8.2 | 827 | 17.1 | — | 3 | E31 k | E18 k |
| Cross-section composite | May 1 2008 | 0945 CST | 740 | 14.5 | E15000 | 11.6 | 8.2 | 873 | 13.6 | — | 3 | 92 | E18 k |
| Cross-section composite | May 7 2008 | 0940 CST | 739 | 15.8 | E15100 | 10.6 | 8.2 | 933 | 17.4 | — | 3 | E26 k | E8 k |
| Cross-section composite | May 21 2008 | 0930 CST | 743 | 11.0 | E14000 | 10.0 | 8.1 | 820 | 16.6 | — | 3 | E14 k | E10 k |
| Cross-section composite | May 28 2008 | 1015 CST | 758 | 13.0 | E13200 | 11.6 | 8.5 | 874 | 18.1 | — | 3 | E23 k | E23 k |
| Cross-section composite | June 12 2008 | 0805 CDT | 747 | 24.0 | E28200 | — | 7.9 | — | 23.9 | — | 3 | 90 | E100 k |
| Cross-section composite | July 2 2008 | 0915 CST | 745 | 22.4 | E12700 | 9.6 | 8.3 | 765 | 24.9 | — | 3 | E17 k | E24 k |
| Cross-section composite | July 16 2008 | 1000 CST | 753 | 22.7 | E17200 | 9.0 | 8.3 | 786 | — | — | 3 | E120 k | E100 k |
| Cross-section composite | Aug 20 2008 | 1110 CST | 756 | 25.8 | E6460 | 9.2 | 8.4 | 726 | 27.6 | — | 3 | E10 k | E13 k |
| Cross-section composite | Sept 22 2008 | 1235 CST | 761 | 27.3 | E45100 | 6.2 | 8.0 | 503 | 20.8 | — | 3 | 83 | 80 |

**Table 2.**  Physical, chemical, and bacterial data for the Illinois River below Peoria Lake at Peoria, Illinois (U.S. Geological Survey streamflow-gaging station number 05562200), during water year 2008 (October 2007–September 2008)

[hhmm, hour minute; Hg, mercury; MF, membrane filter; col/100 mL, colonies per 100 milliliters; ft, foot; ft³/s, cubic foot per second; micron, micrometer; mg/L, milligrams per liter; mm, millimeter; C, degrees Celsius; µS/cm, microsiemens per centimeter; —, no data; E, estimated; k, counts outside acceptable range; CDT, central daylight time; CST, central standard time]

| Sample notes | Date | Time (24-hour clock, hhmm) | Barometric pressure (mm Hg) | Temperature, air (°C) | Discharge (ft³/s) | Dissolved oxygen, water, unfiltered (mg/L) | pH, water, unfiltered, field (standard units) | Specific conductance, water, unfiltered (µS/cm at 25 °C) | Temperature, water (°C) | Gage height (ft) | Number of sampling points (count) | Escherichia coli, modified m-TEC MF method, water (col/100 mL) | Fecal coliform, M-FC MF (0.45 micron) method, water (col/100 mL) |
|---|---|---|---|---|---|---|---|---|---|---|---|---|---|
| | | | (00025) | (00020) | (00060) | (00300) | (00400) | (00095) | (00010) | (00065) | (00063) | (90902) | (31616) |
| Synoptic sample, mid-channel | Oct 10 2007 | 1210 CDT | — | E10.8 | E6760 | — | — | — | — | — | 1 | 130 | 300 |
| | Oct 18 2007 | 1220 CST | 725 | — | E6000 | 8.2 | 8.1 | 838 | 18.2 | — | 1 | 750 | 1100 |
| | Oct 25 2007 | 0915 CST | 752 | 4.4 | E10200 | 9.8 | 8.3 | 868 | 12.3 | — | 1 | 53 | 88 |
| | Nov 1 2007 | 0945 CST | 757 | 7.2 | E8970 | 9.9 | 8.0 | 865 | 12.2 | — | 1 | 43 | 120 |
| | Nov 7 2007 | 1110 CST | 756 | 2.8 | E7370 | 11.3 | 8.1 | 805 | 7.9 | — | 1 | 110 | 200 |
| | Nov 15 2007 | 1030 CST | 751 | 4.4 | E7070 | 12.0 | 8.4 | 805 | 9.4 | — | 1 | 450 | 340 |
| | Nov 21 2007 | 1020 CST | 744 | — | E7550 | 12.5 | 8.9 | 833 | 10.0 | — | 1 | E9700 k | E6800 k |
| | Nov 28 2007 | 0845 CST | 748 | 4.4 | E12000 | 13.1 | 8.5 | 871 | 3.7 | — | 1 | 200 | E250 k |
| | Dec 5 2007 | 0800 CST | 743 | 0.0 | E15500 | 13.6 | 8.4 | 818 | 1.1 | — | 1 | 77 | 76 |
| | Dec 12 2007 | 0800 CST | 754 | -1.1 | E13600 | 14.0 | 8.3 | 826 | 0.8 | — | 1 | 88 | 40 |
| | Dec 19 2007 | 0755 CST | 749 | -4.4 | E26200 | 14.1 | 8.0 | 855 | 1.2 | — | 1 | 140 | 210 |
| | Jan 3 2008 | 0815 CST | 764 | -10.0 | E22100 | 13.9 | 7.5 | 888 | 0.0 | — | 1 | 220 | 200 |
| | Jan 9 2008 | 0800 CST | 750 | 1.3 | E28900 | 12.7 | 8.1 | 982 | 4.7 | — | 1 | 79 | 130 |

**Table 2.** Physical, chemical, and bacterial data for the Illinois River below Peoria Lake at Peoria, Illinois (U.S. Geological Survey streamflow-gaging station number 05562200), during water year 2008 (October 2007–September 2008).—Continued

[hhmm, hour minute; Hg, mercury; MF, membrane filter; col/100 mL, colonies per 100 milliliters; ft, foot; ft³/s, cubic foot per second; micron, micrometer; mg/L, milligrams per liter; mm, millimeter; C, degrees Celsius; µS/cm, microsiemens per centimeter; —, no data; E, estimated; k, counts outside acceptable range; CDT, central daylight time; CST, central standard time]

Data Collection   11

| Sample notes | Date | Time (24-hour clock, hhmm) | Barometric pressure (mm Hg) (00025) | Temperature, air (°C) (00020) | Discharge (ft³/s) (00060) | Dissolved oxygen, water, unfiltered (mg/L) (00300) | pH, water, unfiltered, field (standard units) (00400) | Specific conductance, water, unfiltered (µS/cm at 25 °C) (00095) | Temperature, water (°C) (00010) | Gage height (ft) (00065) | Number of sampling points (count) (00063) | Escherichia coli, modified m-TEC MF method, water (col/100 mL) (90902) | Fecal coliform, M-FC MF (0.45 micron) method, water (col/100 mL) (31616) |
|---|---|---|---|---|---|---|---|---|---|---|---|---|---|
| | Jan 16 2008 | 0750 CST | 748 | -2.0 | E59400 | 10.9 | 7.9 | 591 | 2.9 | — | 1 | 190 | 130 |
| | Jan 24 2008 | 0820 CST | 757 | -20.5 | E33800 | 11.7 | 7.8 | 519 | 0.0 | — | 1 | 110 | 93 |
| Runoff/snowmelt event | Feb 6 2008 | 0715 CST | 734 | 0.0 | E27900 | 11.8 | 8.0 | 734 | 0.1 | — | 1 | 1900 | E2250 k |
| | Mar 12 2008 | 0805 CST | 744 | 0.0 | E35100 | 12.3 | 8.4 | 843 | 2.7 | — | 1 | E26 k | E18 k |
| | Mar 26 2008 | 0740 CST | 751 | 2.0 | E30600 | 12.9 | 8.3 | 813 | 6.5 | — | 1 | E31 k | E24 k |
| | Apr 2 2008 | 0740 CST | 758 | 2.0 | E33400 | 11.8 | 8.4 | 938 | 7.6 | — | 1 | E15 k | E4 k |
| | Apr 9 2008 | 0740 CST | 751 | 4.7 | E32100 | 11.0 | 8.3 | 903 | 10.3 | — | 1 | E7 k | E5 k |
| | Apr 16 2008 | 0740 CST | 747 | 8.5 | E35300 | 11.3 | 8.2 | 867 | 9.7 | — | 1 | E10 k | E10 k |
| | Apr 23 2008 | 0735 CST | 753 | 14.8 | E30600 | 10.5 | 8.2 | 809 | 16.7 | — | 1 | E2 k | E3 k |
| | May 1 2008 | 0735 CST | 740 | 14.5 | E26500 | 10.8 | 8.2 | 828 | 14.7 | — | 1 | E7 k | E3 k |
| | May 7 2008 | 0740 CST | 740 | 16.0 | E21400 | 11.9 | 8.6 | 865 | 17.5 | — | 1 | E14 k | E5 k |
| | May 21 2008 | 0730 CST | 741 | 10.4 | E24400 | 11.6 | 8.6 | 781 | 16.3 | — | 1 | E4 k | E1 k |
| | May 28 2008 | 0725 CST | 757 | 9.4 | E19800 | 9.3 | 8.9 | 812 | 16.1 | — | 1 | E9 k | E9 k |

**Table 2.** Physical, chemical, and bacterial data for the Illinois River below Peoria Lake at Peoria, Illinois (U.S. Geological Survey streamflow-gaging station number 05562200), during water year 2008 (October 2007–September 2008).—Continued

[hhmm, hour minute; Hg, mercury; MF, membrane filter; col/100 mL, colonies per 100 milliliters; ft, foot; ft³/s, cubic foot per second; micron, micrometer; mg/L, milligrams per liter; mm, millimeter; C, degrees Celsius; µS/cm, microsiemens per centimeter; —, no data; E, estimated; k, counts outside acceptable range; CDT, central daylight time; CST, central standard time]

| Sample notes | Date | Time (24-hour clock, hhmm) | Barometric pressure (mm Hg) | Temperature, air (°C) | Discharge (ft³/s) | Dissolved oxygen, water, unfiltered (mg/L) | pH, water, unfiltered, field (standard units) | Specific conductance, water, unfiltered (µS/cm at 25 °C) | Temperature, water (°C) | Gage height (ft) | Number of sampling points (count) | Escherichia coli, modified m-TEC MF method, water (col/100 mL) | Fecal coliform, M-FC MF (0.45 micron) method, water (col/100 mL) |
|---|---|---|---|---|---|---|---|---|---|---|---|---|---|
| | | | (00025) | (00020) | (00060) | (00300) | (00400) | (00095) | (00010) | (00065) | (00063) | (90902) | (31616) |
| Synoptic sample, mid-channel | June 12 2008 | 1115 CDT | 752 | E29 2 | E20400 | 7.0 | 8.0 | 620 | 24.1 | — | 3 | 120 | 410 |
| | July 2 2008 | 0750 CST | 746 | 21.0 | E15900 | 7.8 | 8.2 | 728 | 25.1 | — | 1 | E19 k | E4 k |
| | July 16 2008 | 0720 CST | 753 | 23.0 | E18600 | 7.2 | 8.4 | 658 | 26.7 | — | 1 | 63 | E100 k |
| | Aug 20 2008 | 0830 CST | 752 | 20.8 | E7240 | 7.3 | 8.4 | 703 | 26.2 | — | 1 | 80 | 110 |
| | Sept 22 2008 | 0945 CST | 758 | 22.8 | E67100 | 4.4 | 8.1 | 380 | 20.5 | — | 1 | 38 | 110 |

**Table 3.** Physical, chemical, and bacterial data for Big Bureau Creek near Princeton, Illinois (U.S. Geological Survey streamflow-gaging station number 05556500), during water year 2008 (October 2007–September 2008).

[hhmm, hour minute; Hg, mercury; MF, membrane filter; col/100 mL, colonies per 100 milliliters; ft, foot; ft³/s, cubic foot per second; micron, micrometer; mg/L, milligrams per liter; mm, millimeter; C, degrees Celsius; µS/cm, microsiemens per centimeter; —, no data; E, estimated; k, counts outside acceptable range; CDT, central daylight time; CST, central standard time]

| Sample notes | Date | Time (24-hour clock, hhmm) | Barometric pressure (mm Hg) (00025) | Temperature, air (°C) (00020) | Discharge instantaneous (ft³/s) (00061) | Dissolved oxygen, water, unfiltered (mg/L) (00300) | pH, water, unfiltered, field (standard units) (00400) | Specific conductance, water, unfiltered (µS/cm at 25 °C) (00095) | Temperature, water (°C) (00010) | Gage height (ft) (00065) | Number of sampling points (count) (00063) | Escherichia coli, modified m-TEC MF method, water (col/100 mL) (90902) | Fecal coliform, M-FC MF (0.45 micron) method, water (col/100 mL) (31616) |
|---|---|---|---|---|---|---|---|---|---|---|---|---|---|
| Sampled near mouth, no sample at this location | Oct 10 2007 | — | — | — | — | — | — | — | — | — | — | — | — |
|  | Nov 1 2007 | 1250 CST | 753 | 12.8 | 26 | 13.1 | 8.4 | 781 | 9.5 | 1.55 | 1 | 65 | 220 |
|  | Dec 5 2007 | 1200 CST | 743 | -1.1 | 46 | 14.4 | 8.4 | 770 | 0.2 | 1.75 | 1 | 100 | 33 |
|  | Jan 9 2008 | 1020 CST | 747 | 1.0 | 885 | 11.6 | 8.0 | 682 | 5.1 | 4.71 | 1 | 1200 | E900 k |
| Runoff/snowmelt event | Feb 6 2008 | 0920 CST | 730 | 0.0 | 273 | 12.9 | 8.1 | 667 | 0.2 | 3.06 | 1 | 1700 | 1920 |
|  | Mar 12 2008 | 1030 CST | 742 | 3.4 | 939 | 11.8 | 8.2 | 350 | 1.9 | 4.83 | 1 | 280 | E280 k |
|  | Apr 9 2008 | 1000 CST | 748 | 3.8 | 258 | 11.4 | 8.2 | 667 | 7.3 | 2.98 | 1 | 870 | 900 |
|  | May 21 2008 | 1005 CST | 741 | 10.9 | 187 | 11.3 | 8.1 | 683 | 13.5 | 2.66 | 1 | 120 | 110 |
| Synoptic sample | June 12 2008 | 0835 CDT | 744 | 19.0 | 282 | 8.8 | 8.2 | 696 | 18.5 | 3.07 | 1 | 440 | 450 |
|  | July 16 2008 | 0915 CST | 749 | 23.1 | 405 | 8.4 | 8.1 | 663 | 21.2 | 3.49 | 1 | 1100 | 1170 |
|  | Aug 20 2008 | 1035 CST | 751 | 21.1 | 25 | 8.9 | 8.1 | 647 | 23.5 | 1.56 | 1 | 740 | 580 |
|  | Sept 22 2008 | 1155 CST | 755 | 25.3 | 291 | 9.0 | 8.1 | 672 | 18.6 | 3.10 | 1 | 610 | 510 |

**Table 4.** Physical, chemical, and bacterial data for Farm Creek at Farmdale, Illinois (U.S. Geological Survey streamflow-gaging station number 05560500), during water year 2008 (October 2007–September 2008)

[hhmm, hour minute; Hg, mercury; MF, membrane filter; col/100 mL, colonies per 100 milliliters; ft, foot; ft³/s, cubic foot per second; micron, micrometer; mg/L, milligrams per liter; mm, millimeter; C, degrees Celsius; µS/cm, microsiemens per centimeter; —, no data; E, estimated; k, counts outside acceptable range; CDT, central daylight time; CST, central standard time]

| Sample notes | Date | Time (24-hour clock, hhmm) | Baro-metric pressure (mm Hg) | Tempera-ture, air (°C) | Discharge, instanta-neous (ft³/s) | Discharge, (ft³/s) | Dissolved oxygen, water, unfiltered (mg/L) | pH, water, unfiltered, field (standard units) | Specific conductance, water, unfiltered (µS/cm at 25 °C) | Tempera-ture, water (°C) | Gage height (ft) | Number of sampling points (count) | Escherichia coli, modified m-TEC MF method, water (col/100 mL) | Fecal coliform, M-FC MF (0.45 micron) method, water (col/100 mL) |
|---|---|---|---|---|---|---|---|---|---|---|---|---|---|---|
| | | | (00025) | (00020) | (00061) | (00060) | (00300) | (00400) | (00095) | (00010) | (00065) | (00063) | (90902) | (31616) |
| Sampled near mouth, no sample at this location | Oct 10 2007 | — | — | — | — | — | — | — | — | — | — | — | — | — |
| | Nov 1 2007 | 1430 CST | 753 | 12.8 | 2.7 | — | 12.9 | 8.4 | 1480 | 10.7 | 1.90 | 1 | E26 k | 52 |
| | Dec 5 2007 | 1205 CST | 746 | 0.0 | 3.7 | — | 15.8 | 8.7 | 1440 | 2.7 | 1.93 | 1 | 360 | 250 |
| | Jan 9 2008 | 1230 CST | 748 | 4.1 | 402 | — | 11.8 | 7.9 | 535 | 6.1 | 4.00 | 1 | 3400 | — |
| Runoff/snowmelt event | Feb 6 2008 | 1145 CST | 729 | 0.0 | 679 | — | 13.6 | 8.0 | 336 | 0.5 | 4.61 | 1 | E20000 k | E10300 k |
| | Mar 12 2008 | 1235 CST | 744 | 7.4 | 22 | — | 12.0 | 8.2 | 913 | 5.6 | 2.24 | 1 | 210 | 88 |
| | Apr 9 2008 | 1205 CST | 750 | 7.5 | 38 | — | 12.7 | 8.2 | 722 | 9.5 | 2.44 | 1 | 1400 | 2300 |
| | May 21 2008 | 1200 CST | 741 | 13.9 | — | 8.8 | 13.3 | 8.4 | 890 | 15.2 | 2.01 | 1 | E28 k | E26 k |
| Synoptic sample | June 12 2008 | 0640 CDT | 745 | 18.0 | 19 | — | 8.7 | 8.0 | 895 | 18.5 | 2.19 | 1 | 7300 | 1030 |
| | July 16 2008 | 1140 CDT | 752 | 24.6 | 22 | — | 8.5 | 8.2 | 977 | 23.3 | 2.17 | 1 | 1200 | 833 |
| | Aug 20 2008 | 1320 CST | 750 | 24.9 | 2.8 | — | 11.1 | 8.3 | 1940 | 23.5 | 1.74 | 1 | 110 | 120 |
| | Sept 22 2008 | 0820 CST | 754 | 18.6 | 33 | — | 9.3 | 8.7 | 815 | 16.7 | 2.38 | 1 | 1700 | 1130 |

**Table 5.** Physical, chemical, and bacterial data for Senachwine Creek at Chillicothe, Illinois (U.S. Geological Survey streamflow-gaging station number 05559700), during water year 2008 (October 2007–September 2008).

[hhmm, hour minute; Hg, mercury; MF, membrane filter; col/100 mL, colonies per 100 milliliters; ft, foot; ft³/s, cubic foot per second; micron, micrometer; mg/L, milligrams per liter; mm, millimeter; C, degrees Celsius; µS/cm, microsiemens per centimeter; —, no data; E, estimated; k, counts outside acceptable range; CDT, central daylight time; CST, central standard time]

| Sample notes | Date | Time (24-hour clock, hhmm) | Baro-metric pressure (mm Hg) | Tempera-ture, air (°C) | Discharge, instanta-neous (ft³/s) | Discharge (ft³/s) | Dissolved oxygen, water, unfiltered (mg/L) | pH, water, unfiltered, field (standard units) | Specific conductance, water, unfiltered (µS/cm at 25 °C) | Tem-perature, water (°C) | Gage height (ft) | Number of sampling points (count) | Escherichia coli, modified m-TEC MF method, water (col/100 mL) | Fecal coliform, M-FC MF (0.45 micron) method, water (col/100 mL) |
|---|---|---|---|---|---|---|---|---|---|---|---|---|---|---|
| | | | (00025) | (00020) | (00061) | (00060) | (00300) | (00400) | (00095) | (00010) | (00065) | (00063) | (90902) | (31616) |
| No sample, dry | Oct 10 2007 | — | — | — | — | — | — | — | — | — | — | — | — | — |
| No sample, dry | Nov 1 2007 | — | — | — | — | — | — | — | — | — | — | — | — | — |
| | Dec 12 2007 | 0925 CST | 754 | -1.1 | — | E1.7 | 13.1 | 8.2 | 680 | 0.8 | 5.81 | 1 | 63 | E19 k |
| | Jan 9 2008 | 0920 CST | 750 | 0.0 | 182 | — | 12.4 | 8.2 | 603 | 4.2 | 7.95 | 1 | 340 | E180 k |
| Runoff/snowmelt event | Feb 6 2008 | 0820 CST | 732 | 0.0 | — | E190 | 13.4 | 8.1 | 287 | 0.0 | 9.42 | 1 | 1300 | 2000 |
| | Mar 12 2008 | 0935 CST | 745 | 3.8 | 45 | — | 12.7 | 8.3 | 691 | 2.4 | 6.74 | 1 | E11 k | E9 k |
| | Apr 9 2008 | 0910 CST | 750 | 3.7 | 90 | — | 11.1 | 8.3 | 619 | 7.3 | 7.32 | 1 | 600 | 380 |
| | May 21 2008 | 1110 CST | 743 | 12.2 | 44 | — | 11.6 | 8.2 | 673 | 15.4 | 6.73 | 1 | 120 | 65 |
| Synoptic sample | Jun 12 2008 | 1010 CDT | 748 | 22.5 | 40 | — | 9.4 | 8.2 | 706 | 21.3 | 6.68 | 1 | 260 | 430 |
| | Jul 16 2008 | 0820 CST | 752 | 22.3 | 16 | — | 7.9 | 8.1 | 680 | 23.4 | 6.42 | 1 | 300 | 370 |
| No sample, dry | Aug 20 2008 | — | — | — | — | — | — | — | — | — | — | — | — | — |
| | Sep 22 2008 | 1105 CST | 758 | 25.0 | 26 | — | 9.3 | 8.0 | 732 | 18.8 | 6.65 | 1 | 520 | 440 |

**Table 6.** Physical, chemical, and bacterial data for Partridge Creek near Metamora, Illinois (U.S. Geological Survey (USGS) streamflow-gaging station number 05559800), and Partridge Creek Tributary near Metamora, Illinois (USGS streamflow-gaging station number 05559820), from May to August 2008.

[hhmm, hour minute; Hg, mercury; MF, membrane filter; col/100 mL, colonies per 100 milliliters; ft³/s, cubic foot per second; micron, micrometer; mg/L, milligrams per liter; mm, millimeter; C, degrees Celsius; µS/cm, microsiemens per centimeter; —, no data; <, less than; CDT, central daylight time; CST, central standard time]

| Sample notes | Date | Time (24-hour clock, hhmm) | Barometric pressure (mm Hg) (00025) | Temperature, air (°C) (00020) | Discharge, instantaneous (ft³/s) (00061) | Dissolved oxygen, water, unfiltered (mg/L) (00300) | pH, water, unfiltered, field (standard units) (00400) | Specific conductance, water, unfiltered (µS/cm at 25 °C) (00095) | Temperature, water (°C) (00010) | Number of sampling points (count) (00063) | Escherichia coli, modified m-TEC MF method, water (col/100 mL) (90902) | Fecal coliform, M-FC MF (0.45 micron) method, water (col/100 mL) (31616) |
|---|---|---|---|---|---|---|---|---|---|---|---|---|
| | | | | | Partridge Creek near Metamora (05559800) | | | | | | | |
| | May 28 2008 | 0915 CST | 752 | 9 5 | — | 11.4 | 8.3 | 815 | 11.2 | 1 | 220 | 200 |
| Synoptic sample | June 12 2008 | 0720 CDT | 743 | 18 2 | — | 8.6 | 8.1 | 831 | 18.7 | 1 | 800 | 930 |
| | July 16 2008 | 1105 CST | 750 | 25 1 | — | 8.8 | 8.3 | 766 | 23.1 | 1 | 1900 | 1200 |
| | Aug 20 2008 | 1240 CST | 749 | 25.6 | — | 9.5 | 8.3 | 783 | 22.5 | 1 | 580 | 480 |
| | | | | | Partridge Creek Tributary near Metamora (05559820) | | | | | | | |
| | May 28 2008 | 0900 CST | 752 | 9 5 | — | 11.1 | 8.4 | 770 | 9.9 | 1 | 210 | 150 |
| Synoptic sample | June 12 2008 | 0730 CDT | 743 | 18 2 | — | 8.8 | 8.1 | 774 | 16.9 | 1 | 220 | 1630 |
| | July 16 2008 | 1100 CST | 749 | 25 1 | — | 8.6 | 8.2 | 761 | 21.3 | 1 | 1100 | 900 |
| Near zero flow, no sample possible | Aug 20 2008 | 1230 CDT | 749 | 25.6 | <0.1 | 4.1 | 7.8 | 911 | 16.1 | — | — | — |

## Synoptic Sampling

Intensive synoptic sampling was completed on October 10, 2007, and June 12, 2008. These dates were chosen based on hydrologic conditions in the area at that time. The October 10, 2007, sampling took place during a relatively dry period with streamflows in the Illinois River and tributaries generally at or below the long-term means. In contrast, the June 12, 2008, sampling took place during a relatively wet period with streamflows in the Illinois River and tributaries generally at or above the long-term means (figs. 3 and 4).

During October 2007, samples were collected at 16 sites on the Illinois River and at 14 sites on various tributaries within the study area. The sample sites on the main stem of the Illinois River were selected based mainly on the following factors: the location of major tributary inflows, the location of sewage-treatment plant discharge points, and the location of in-channel lakes where changes in hydraulic characteristics

may affect the transport and (or) lifespan of bacteria. Tributary sample sites were selected to best represent possible bacteria loading from a wide range of land-use areas, ranging from rural to urban. As was the case with the periodic sampling, all samples were analyzed for both FC and *E. coli*, and observations of air temperature, water temperature, barometric pressure, dissolved oxygen, pH, and specific conductance were measured at each sampling location. Streamflow is estimated at sites without continuous monitoring. Results of the October 10, 2007, sampling are presented in table 7.

During June 2008, samples were collected at 12 sites on the Illinois River and at 5 sites on tributaries within the study area. These sites were a subset of the sites that were sampled in October 2007; the results of the October 2007 sampling indicated that a similar amount of information could be obtained while sampling fewer sites throughout the study area. The results of the June 12, 2008, sampling are presented in table 8.

**Table 7.**  Results of synoptic sampling on the Illinois River and selected tributaries between Hennepin and Peoria, Illinois, October 10, 2007.

[hhmm, hour minute; Hg, mercury; MF, membrane filter;  col/100 mL, colonies per 100 milliliters; ft, foot; ft³/s, cubic foot per second; micron, micrometer; mg/L, milligrams per liter; mm, millimeter;  C, degrees Celsius; µS/cm, microsiemens per centimeter; —, no data; <, less than; E, estimated; k, counts outside acceptable range; CDT, central daylight time; CST, central standard time; DS, downstream; US, upstream]

| Site name | U.S. Geological Survey station number | Sample notes | Time (24-hour clock, hhmm) | Barometric pressure (mm Hg) (00025) | Temperature, air (°C) (00020) | Discharge, instantaneous (ft³/s) (00061) | Dissolved oxygen, water, unfiltered (mg/L) (00300) |
|---|---|---|---|---|---|---|---|
| Illinois River Upstream of Hennepin near Mile 209.3 | | Mid-channel grab | 1420 CDT | 749 | E13.0 | — | 9.8 |
| Illinois River Upstream of Hennepin near Mile 208.4 | | Mid-channel grab | 1430 CDT | 749 | E12.5 | — | 9.6 |
| Illinois River at Hennepin | 05556200 | Cross-section part 1 of 4; Collected near right-channel | 1435 CDT | 749 | E12.5 | — | 10.0 |
| | | Cross-section part 2 of 4; Collected near mid-channel | 1440 CDT | 750 | E12.0 | — | 9.1 |
| | | Cross-section part 3 of 4; Collected near island, navigation-channel side | 1445 CDT | 748 | E12.0 | — | 8.9 |
| | | Cross-section part 4 of 4; Collected sample near left-channel | 1450 CDT | 748 | E12.0 | — | 9.4 |
| Illinois River Upstream of Henry near Mile 198.2 | | Mid-channel grab | 1310 CDT | — | E13.0 | — | — |
| Illinois River at Henry | 05558300 | Mid-channel grab | 1255 CDT | — | E13.0 | 7510 | — |
| Illinois River at Lacon | 05558995 | Mid-channel grab | 1230 CDT | — | E13.0 | — | — |
| Illinois River Downstream of Lacon near Mile 188.7 | | Collected sample near left-bank | 1225 CDT | — | E12.5 | — | — |
| Illinois River at Chillicothe | 05559600 | Mid-channel grab, at public boat ramp | 1631 CDT | 748 | E12.1 | — | 8.4 |
| Illinois River downstream of Chillicothe near Mile 179 | | Collected sample near right-bank | 1555 CDT | — | E12.1 | — | — |
| | | Mid-channel grab | 1600 CDT | — | E12.1 | — | — |
| Illinois River at South Rome | 05559850 | Mid-channel grab | 1545 CDT | E748 | E53.8 | — | |

| pH, water, unfiltered, field (standard units) (00400) | Specific conductance, water, unfiltered (µS/cm at 25 °C) (00095) | Temperature, water (°C) (00010) | Gage height (ft) (00065) | Sampling depth (ft) (00003) | Number of sampling points (count) (00063) | *Escherichia coli*, modified m-TEC MF method, water (col/100 mL) (90902) | Fecal coliform, M-FC MF (0.45 micron) method, water (col/100 mL) (31616) |
|---|---|---|---|---|---|---|---|
| 8.5 | 852 | 21.9 | — | 3.00 | 1 | E17 k | 50 |
| 8.5 | 974 | 22.4 | — | 3.00 | 1 | E13 k | E30 k |
| 8.6 | 849 | 21.8 | — | 3.00 | 1 | E10 k | 52 |
| 8.5 | 850 | 21.9 | — | 3.00 | 1 | E16 k | E20 k |
| 8.5 | 850 | 21.8 | — | 3.00 | 1 | E13 k | E18 k |
| 8.5 | 894 | 21.8 | — | 2.00 | 1 | 770 | E36 k |
| — | — | — | — | 3.00 | 1 | 38 | 45 |
| — | — | — | 14.73 | 3.00 | 1 | E13 k | 40 |
| — | — | — | — | 3.00 | 1 | E8 k | E6 k |
| — | — | — | — | 2.00 | 1 | 73 | 98 |
| 8.5 | 836 | 20.8 | — | 3.00 | 1 | E2 k | E12 k |
| — | — | 20.6 | — | 2.00 | 1 | 45 | 430 |
| — | — | 20.6 | — | 3.00 | 1 | E2 k | E9 k |
| 8.5 | 832 | 20.6 | | 3.00 | 1 | E12 k | E24 k |

**Table 7.**   Results of synoptic sampling on the Illinois River and selected tributaries between Hennepin and Peoria, Illinois, October 10, 2007.—Continued

[hhmm, hour minute; Hg, mercury; MF, membrane filter;  col/100 mL, colonies per 100 milliliters; ft, foot; ft³/s, cubic foot per second; micron, micrometer; mg/L, milligrams per liter; mm, millimeter;  C, degrees Celsius; µS/cm, microsiemens per centimeter; —, no data; <, less than; E, estimated; k, counts outside acceptable range; CDT, central daylight time; CST, central standard time; DS, downstream; US, upstream]

| Site name | U.S. Geological Survey station number | Sample notes | Time (24-hour clock, hhmm) | Barometric pressure (mm Hg) (00025) | Temperature, air (°C) (00020) | Discharge, instantaneous (ft³/s) (00061) | Dissolved oxygen, water, unfiltered (mg/L) (00300) |
|---|---|---|---|---|---|---|---|
| Illinois River at Water Company at Peoria | 05559900 | Mid-channel grab | 0845 CDT | — | E8.8 | — | — |
|  |  | Collected sample near right-bank | 0850 CDT | — | E8.8 | — | — |
| Illinois River at Peoria | 05560000 | Cross-section part 1 of 3; near Mile 163, left-channel | 1245 CDT | — | E11.7 | — | — |
|  |  | Cross-section part 2 of 3; near Mile 163, mid-channel | 1250 CDT | — | E11.7 | — | — |
|  |  | Cross-section part 3 of 3; near Mile 163, right-channel | 1255 CDT | — | E11.7 | — | — |
| Illinois River at William Kumpf Blvd at Peoria | 05562100 | Mid-channel grab | 1240 CDT | — | E11.2 | — | — |
| Illinois River upstream of Highway 8/29/116 Bridge at Peoria |  | Mid-channel grab | 1235 CDT | — | E11.2 | — | — |
| Illinois River near railroad bridge at Peoria near Mile 160.8 |  | Collected sample near right-bank | 1225 CDT | — | E11.2 | — | — |
| Illinois River below Peoria Lake at Peoria | 05562200 | Mid-channel grab | 1210 CDT | — | E10.8 | — | — |
|  |  | Collected sample near right-bank | 1215 CDT | — | E10.9 | — | — |
| Big Bureau Creek at Bureau | 05558000 | Mid-channel grab | 0900 CDT | 749 | 13.0 | 115 | 8.4 |
| Sandy Creek at Henry | 05558295 | Mid-channel grab | 0945 CDT | 748 | E10.0 | 16 | 9.1 |
| Crow Creek (West) at Highway 29 near Sparland |  | Mid-channel grab | 0950 CDT | 749 | E10.0 | <.10 | 2.9 |
| Thenius Creek at Sparland | 05558990 | Mid-channel grab | 1115 CDT | 749 | E10.5 | .10 | 7.6 |
| Crow Creek near Chillicothe | 05559590 | Mid-channel grab | 0840 CDT | 747 | E9.0 | 10 | 7.1 |

| pH, water, unfiltered, field (standard units) (00400) | Specific conductance, water, unfiltered (µS/cm at 25 °C) (00095) | Tem-pera-ture, water (°C) (00010) | Gage height (ft) (00065) | Sampling depth (ft) (00003) | Number of sampling points (count) (00063) | *Escherichia coli*, modified m-TEC MF method, water (col/100 mL) (90902) | Fecal coliform, M-FC MF (0.45 micron) method, water (col/100 mL) (31616) |
|---|---|---|---|---|---|---|---|
| — | — | 18.3 | — | 3.00 | 1 | E15 k | E5 k |
| — | — | 18.3 | — | 2.00 | 1 | E5 k | E4 k |
| — | — | 18.3 | — | 3.00 | 1 | E8 k | 43 |
| — | — | 18.3 | — | 3.00 | 1 | E24 k | 180 |
| — | — | 18.9 | — | 3.00 | 1 | 30 | 160 |
| — | — | 18.9 | — | 3.00 | 1 | 370 | 94 |
| — | — | 19.4 | — | 3.00 | 1 | 93 | 190 |
| — | — | 20.0 | — | 3.00 | 1 | 570 | 870 |
| — | — | — | — | 3.00 | 1 | 130 | 300 |
| — | — | 20.0 | — | 3.00 | 1 | 130 | 240 |
| 7.8 | 719 | 13.8 | — | .50 | 1 | 200 | 200 |
| — | 726 | 14.2 | — | 1.50 | 1 | 260 | 410 |
| 7.7 | 811 | 14.7 | — | .50 | 1 | E5 k | E6 k |
| 7.8 | 903 | 14.3 | — | — | 1 | 90 | 220 |
| — | 704 | 11.6 | — | 1.50 | 1 | 160 | 150 |

**Table 7.**  Results of synoptic sampling on the Illinois River and selected tributaries between Hennepin and Peoria, Illinois, October 10, 2007.—Continued

[hhmm, hour minute; Hg, mercury; MF, membrane filter;  col/100 mL, colonies per 100 milliliters; ft, foot; ft³/s, cubic foot per second; micron, micrometer; mg/L, milligrams per liter; mm, millimeter;  C, degrees Celsius; µS/cm, microsiemens per centimeter; —, no data; <, less than; E, estimated; k, counts outside acceptable range; CDT, central daylight time; CST, central standard time; DS, downstream; US, upstream]

| Site name | U.S. Geological Survey station number | Sample notes | Time (24-hour clock, hhmm) | Barometric pressure (mm Hg) (00025) | Temperature, air (°C) (00020) | Discharge, instantaneous (ft³/s) (00061) | Dissolved oxygen, water, unfiltered (mg/L) (00300) |
|---|---|---|---|---|---|---|---|
| Senachwine Creek at Chillicothe | 05559700 | No sample, dry | | — | — | — | — |
| Richland Creek below Dry Creek Mouth near Chillicothe | 05559770 | Mid-channel grab | 0745 CDT | 745 | E7.3 | .71 | 6.2 |
| Partridge Creek near Spring Bay | 05559830 | Mid-channel grab | 1420 CDT | 749 | E12.6 | .46 | 9.8 |
| Blalock Creek near Spring Bay | 05559840 | Mid-channel grab | 1355 CDT | 749 | E12.8 | .02 | 7.8 |
| Tenmile Creek at Trailpark Gardens | 05559890 | Mid-channel grab | 1320 CDT | 749 | E12.1 | 1.3 | 10.1 |
| Farm Creek at U.S. Highway 150 at East Peoria | 05561800 | Mid-channel grab | 1215 CDT | 749 | 12.5 | .43 | 18.4 |
| Farm Creek at East Peoria | 05562000 | Mid-channel grab | 1120 CDT | 750 | E10.9 | <1.0 | 19.3 |
| Farm Creek at Camp Street Bridge at East Peoria | 05562010 | Mid-channel grab | 1045 CDT | 749 | E10.8 | <1.0 | 16.6 |
| Kickapoo Creek at Bartonville | 05563525 | Mid-channel grab about 150ft US of HWY24 | 0825 CDT | 748 | E8.3 | 4.1 | 7.7 |
| | | Mid-channel grab about 1500ft DS of HWY24 | 0805 CDT | 749 | E7.8 | 4.1 | 10.0 |

| pH, water, unfiltered, field (standard units) (00400) | Specific conductance, water, unfiltered (μS/cm at 25 °C) (00095) | Temperature, water (°C) (00010) | Gage height (ft) (00065) | Sampling depth (ft) (00003) | Number of sampling points (count) (00063) | *Escherichia coli*, modified m-TEC MF method, water (col/100 mL) (90902) | Fecal coliform, M-FC MF (0.45 micron) method, water (col/100 mL) (31616) |
|---|---|---|---|---|---|---|---|
| — | — | — | — | — | — | — | — |
| — | 743 | 14.4 | — | .20 | 1 | 770 | 970 |
| — | 658 | 17.1 | — | 1.00 | 1 | E21 k | E34 k |
| — | 774 | 14.5 | — | .30 | 1 | 740 | 610 |
| — | 781 | 14.6 | — | .70 | 1 | 410 | 6 |
| — | 1410 | 15.5 | — | .40 | 1 | 270 | 800 |
| — | 1230 | 14.4 | — | .20 | 1 | 73 | 83 |
| — | 1290 | 13.3 | — | E.60 | 1 | 110 | 140 |
| — | 962 | 15.0 | — | E.60 | 1 | 110 | 290 |
| — | 991 | 14.9 | — | E.80 | 1 | E740 k | 390 |

**Table 8.**   Results of synoptic sampling on the Illinois River and selected tributaries between Hennepin and Peoria, Illinois, June 12, 2008.

[hhmm, hour minute; Hg, mercury; MF, membrane filter; col/100 mL, colonies per 100 milliliters; ft, foot; ft³/s, cubic foot per second; micron, micrometer; mg/L, milligrams per liter; mm, millimeter;  C, degrees Celsius; µS/cm, microsiemens per centimeter; —, no data; <, less than; E, estimated; k, counts outside acceptable range; CDT, central daylight time; CST, central standard time]

| Site name | U.S. Geological Survey station number | Sample notes | Time (24-hour clock, hhmm) | Barometric pressure (mm Hg) (00025) | Temperature, air (°C) (00020) | Discharge, instantaneous (ft³/s) (00061) |
|---|---|---|---|---|---|---|
| Illinois River at Hennepin | 05556200 | Cross-section composite | 0805 CDT | 747 | 24.0 | — |
| Illinois River at Henry | 05558300 | Mid-channel grab | 0910 CDT | 747 | 25.0 | 28500 |
| Illinois River at Lacon | 05558995 | Mid-channel grab | 1000 CDT | 747 | 25.0 | — |
| Illinois River at Chillicothe | 05559600 | Mid-channel grab, at public boat ramp | 1055 CDT | 748 | 26.5 | — |
| Illinois River at South Rome | 05559850 | Mid-channel grab | 1215 CDT | 748 | 24.5 | — |
| Illinois River at Water Company at Peoria | 05559900 | Mid-channel grab | 0950 CDT | 751 | E26.9 | — |
| Illinois River at Peoria | 05560000 | Cross-section part 3 of 3; near Mile 163, right-channel | 1025 CDT | 750 | E28.0 | — |
|  |  | Cross-section part 2 of 3; near Mile 163, mid-channel | 1030 CDT | 752 | E28.1 | — |
|  |  | Cross-section part 1 of 3; near Mile 163, left-channel | 1040 CDT | 753 | E28.3 | — |
| Illinois River at William Kumpf Blvd at Peoria | 05562100 | Mid-channel grab | 1045 CDT | 751 | E28.5 | — |
| Illinois River upstream of Highway 8/29/116 Bridge at Peoria |  | Mid-channel grab | 1100 CDT | 751 | E28.9 | — |
| Illinois River near railroad bridge at Peoria near Mile 160.8 |  | Mid-channel grab | 1110 CDT | 752 | E29.1 | — |
| Illinois River below Peoria Lake at Peoria | 05562200 | Cross-section composite | 1115 CDT | 752 | E29.2 | — |
| Illinois River above Peoria Lock and Dam near Creve Coeur | 05563590 | Cross-section composite, near Mile 159 | 1135 CDT | 751 | E29.5 | — |
| Big Bureau Creek at Princeton | 05556500 | Mid-channel grab | 0835 CDT | 744 | 19.0 | 282 |
| Senachwine Creek at Chillicothe | 05559700 | Mid-channel grab | 1010 CDT | 748 | 22.5 | 40 |
| Partridge Creek near Metamora | 05559800 | Mid-channel grab | 0720 CDT | 743 | 18.2 | — |
| Partridge Creek Tributary near Metamora | 05559820 | Mid-channel grab | 0730 CDT | 743 | 18.2 | — |
| Farm Creek at Farmdale | 05560500 | Mid-channel grab | 0640 CDT | 745 | 18.0 | 19 |

| Dissolved oxygen, water, unfiltered (mg/L) (00300) | pH, water, unfiltered, field (standard units) (00400) | Specific conductance, water, unfiltered (µS/cm at 25 °C) (00095) | Tem perature, water (°C) (00010) | Gage height (ft) (00065) | Sampling depth (ft) (00003) | Number of sampling points (count) (00063) | *Escherichia coli*, modified m-TEC MF method, water (col/100 mL) (90902) | Fecal coliform, M-FC MF (0.45 micron) method, water (col/100 mL) (31616) |
|---|---|---|---|---|---|---|---|---|
| — | 7.9 | — | 23.9 | — | 3.00 | 3 | 90 | E100 k |
| — | 7.8 | — | 23.5 | 20.64 | 3.00 | 1 | 73 | 110 |
| — | 7.8 | — | 23.7 | — | 3.00 | 1 | 77 | E88 k |
| — | 7.8 | — | 24.1 | — | 3.00 | 1 | 110 | 110 |
| — | 7.9 | — | 24.4 | — | 3.00 | 1 | 78 | 70 |
| 7.1 | 7.9 | 624 | 23.9 | — | 3.00 | 1 | E26 k | 35 |
| 7.0 | 8.0 | 619 | 24.1 | — | 3.00 | 1 | 55 | 35 |
| 7.3 | 8.1 | 620 | 23.9 | — | 3.00 | 1 | E28 k | 45 |
| 7.1 | 8.0 | 619 | 24.1 | — | 3.00 | 1 | E20 k | 71 |
| 7.0 | 8.0 | 618 | 24.1 | — | 3.00 | 1 | E26 k | E44 k |
| 7.0 | 8.0 | 619 | 24.2 | — | 3.00 | 1 | E38 k | E48 k |
| 7.0 | 8.0 | 623 | 24.1 | — | 3.00 | 1 | 190 | 510 |
| 7.0 | 8.0 | 620 | 24.1 | — | 3.00 | 3 | 120 | 410 |
| 6.9 | 8.0 | 623 | 24.2 | — | 3.00 | 3 | 250 | 520 |
| 8.8 | 8.2 | 696 | 18.5 | 3.07 | — | 1 | 440 | 450 |
| 9.4 | 8.2 | 706 | 21.3 | 6.68 | — | 1 | 260 | 430 |
| 8.6 | 8.1 | 831 | 18.7 | — | — | 1 | 800 | 930 |
| 8.8 | 8.1 | 774 | 16.9 | — | — | 1 | 220 | 1630 |
| 8.7 | 8.0 | 895 | 18.5 | 2.19 | — | 1 | 7300 | 1030 |

# Data Analysis

Correlation analyses were performed to investigate the strength of the relation between FC and *E. coli* counts, as well as correlation between each FIB and streamflow. Linear correlation was calculated with Pearson's r coefficient and non-linear correlation with Spearman's rho coefficient, using methods as described in Helsel and Hirsch (1992). Both of these coefficients have the characteristic of ranging in value from −1 to 1. When there is no correlation, the coefficient equals zero. Values closer to 1 indicate both variables increase simultaneously. Values closer to −1 indicate as one variable decreases, the other increases. Statistical significance was chosen for a 90-percent confidence with these tests. This is demonstrated when the p-value is less than 0.1, or 10 percent.

Concentrations of FC and *E. coli* bacteria correlated well with each other for samples from all locations (r = 0.94, p <0.001; fig. 6), for the Illinois River at Hennepin, Ill. (r = 0.95, p <0.001; fig. 7), and for the Illinois River below Peoria Lake at Peoria, Ill. (r = 0.99, p <0.001; fig. 8). Each of these results indicates a strong linear correlation between the concentrations of FC and *E. coli* bacteria. Spearman's rho coefficient was not calculated because of these findings.

Counts of FC bacteria can encompass more types of coliforms than *E. coli* alone; therefore, the possibility exists for an upward counting bias when relying on FC data to indicate potential FIB sources. However, the statistically significant correlation observations may indicate incorporation or substitution of *E. coli* concentrations with those of FC (for non-regulatory purposes) and could be supported for other instances depending on the type of investigation.

Correlation between streamflow and bacteria concentrations also was determined. Weaker relations were found for either FIB to streamflow than were observed between the FIB; however, the correlation coefficients were found to be statistically significant. For both the tributaries and the Illinois River at Hennepin, Ill., a positive coefficient value was found. Interestingly, a negative coefficient was found for both FC and *E. coli* in relation to streamflow for the Illinois River below Peoria Lake at Peoria, Ill.

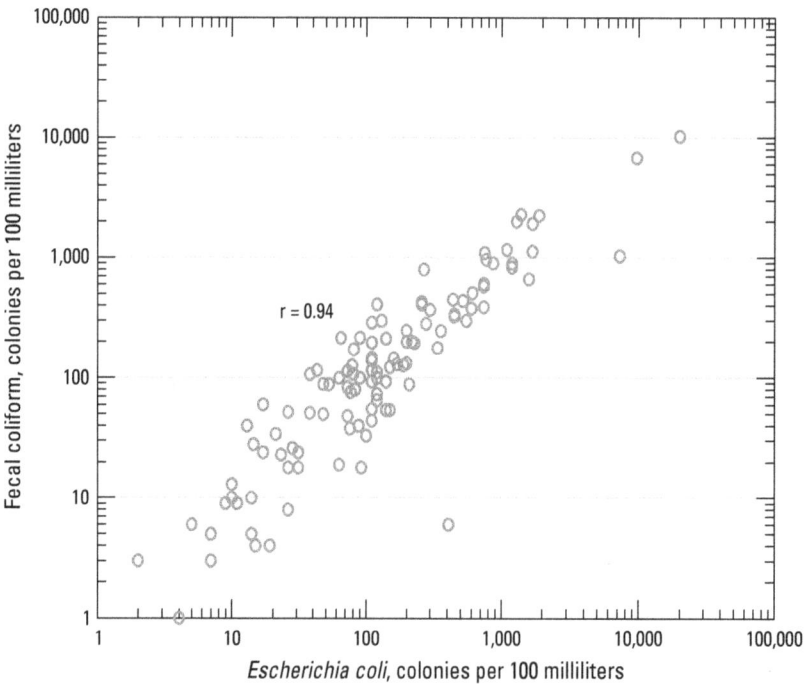

**Figure 6.**   Correlation of fecal coliform to *Escherichia coli* concentrations for all stations and all samples.

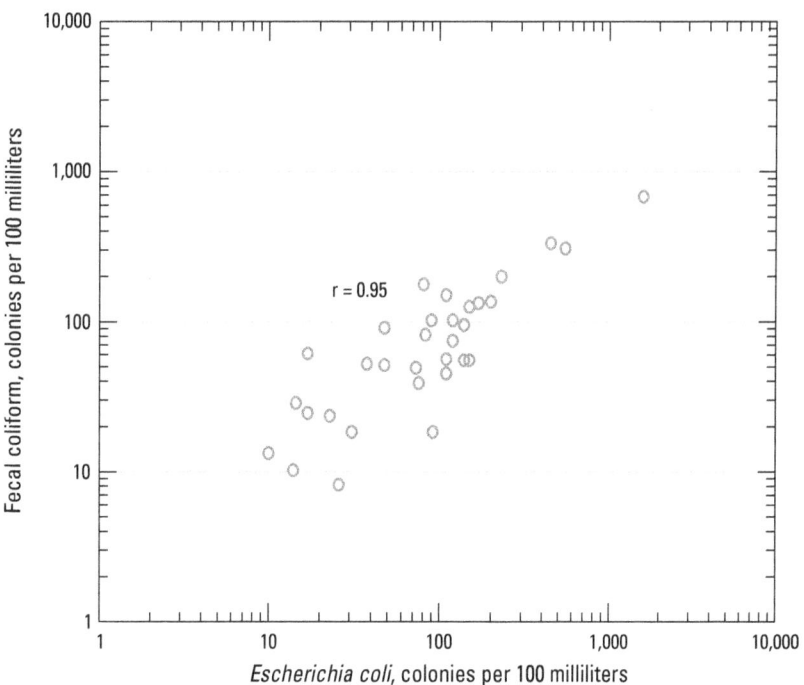

**Figure 7.**    Correlation of fecal coliform to *Escherichia coli* concentrations for Illinois River at Hennepin, Illinois.

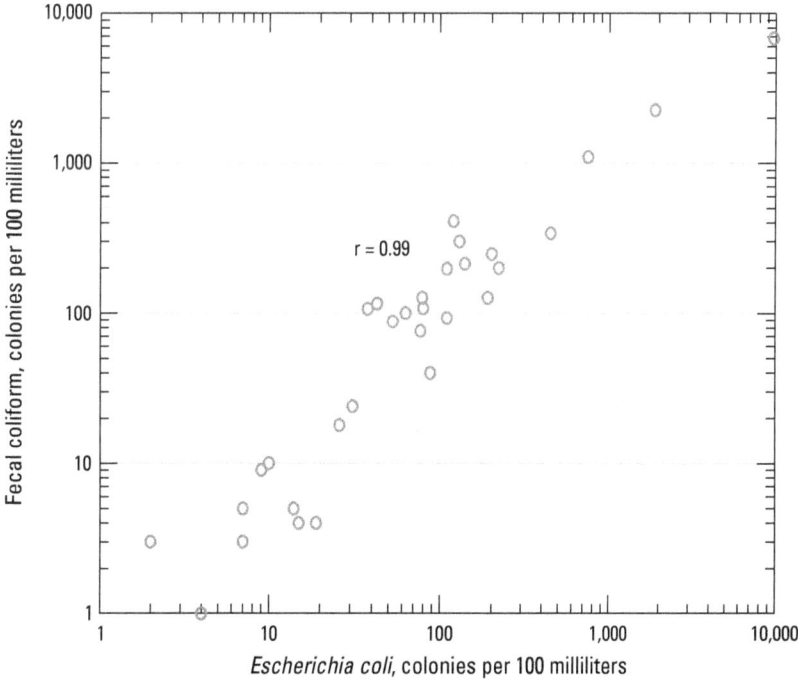

**Figure 8.**    Correlation of fecal coliform to *Escherichia coli* concentrations for Illinois River below Peoria Lake at Peoria, Illinois.

The tributaries to the Illinois River had a weak correlation for streamflow to either FC (rho = 0.40, p = 0.0071; r = 0.44, p = 0.0032) or *E. coli* (rho = 0.48, p = 0.0008; r = 0.40, p = 0.0046), see figure 9. The Illinois River at Hennepin, Ill., had a moderate correlation for streamflow to either FC (rho = 0.49, p = 0.004; r = 0.60, p <0.001) or *E. coli* (rho = 0.66, p <0.001; r = 0.60, p <0.001), see figure 10. The Illinois River below Peoria Lake at Peoria, Ill., had a negative correlation coefficient for streamflow to either FC (rho = −0.44, p = 0.0129) or *E. coli* (rho = −0.43, p = 0.0157), see figure 11. This last relation did not have a statistically significant Pearson r coefficient.

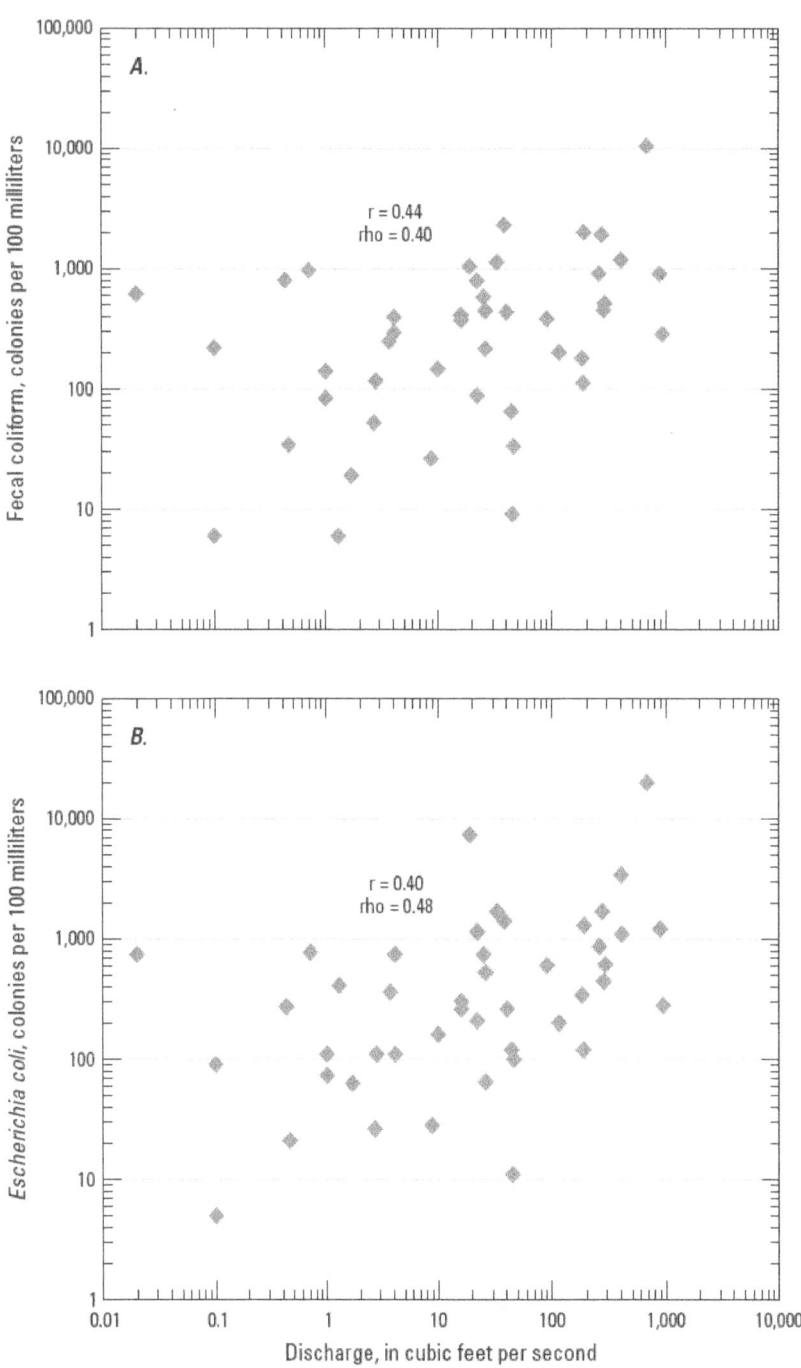

**Figure 9.**    Correlation of *A*, fecal coliform colonies and *B*, *Escherichia coli* colonies to discharge from tributaries to the Illinois River.

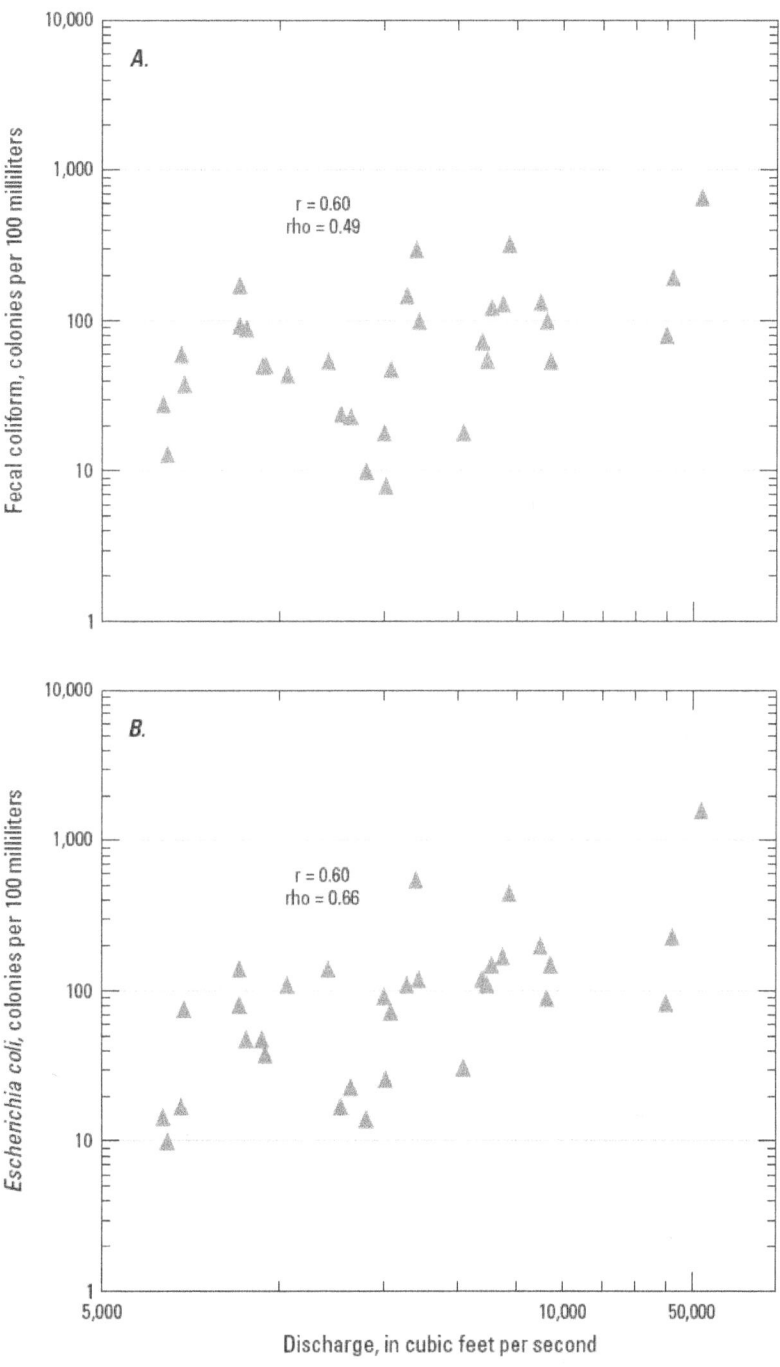

**Figure 10.**   Correlation of *A*, fecal coliform colonies and *B*, *Escherichia coli* colonies to discharge for the Illinois River at Hennepin, Illinois.

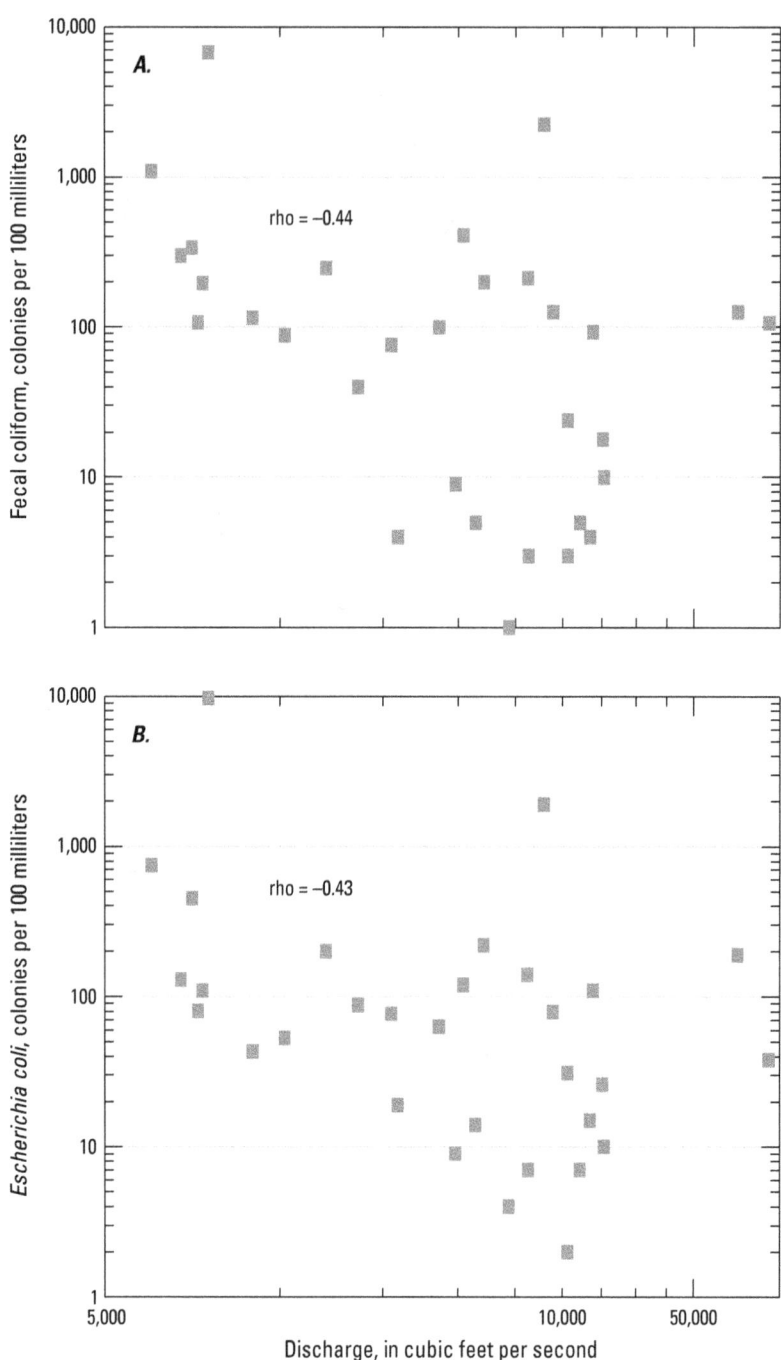

**Figure 11.**    Correlation of *A*, fecal coliform colonies and *B*, *Escherichia coli* colonies to discharge for the Illinois River below Peoria Lake at Peoria, Illinois.

The data from June 2008 indicate a possible influence of CSOs on FC concentrations following rainfall-runoff events in the reach of the Illinois River immediately near Peoria, Ill. The June 2008 synoptic survey of FIB in the Illinois River indicated FC concentrations greater than the water-quality standard only below the known CSO outfalls in Peoria, Ill. Each tributary sampled during June 2008 also had FC concentrations above the standard; however, concentrations in the main stem of the Illinois River below the mouths of these tributaries and still upstream of Peoria, Ill., did not exceed the State of Illinois single-sample water-quality standard of 400 CFU/100 mL. These data are presented in table 8.

The influences of high FIB concentrations in the tributary streams on concentrations in the Illinois River are not clear from the data collected in this investigation. For example, during the June 2008 synoptic sampling, FIB concentrations in Partridge and Farm Creeks exceeded the water-quality standard. These tributaries enter the Illinois River well upstream of the Highway 8/29/116 bridge (figs. 1 and 5); however, FIB concentrations in the Illinois River did not exceed the water-quality standard at any location upstream of the bridge.

# Conclusions

Portions of the Illinois River in Peoria, Woodford, and Tazewell Counties, Illinois, are designated as impaired for primary-contact recreation by the Illinois Environmental Protection Agency, and fecal coliform bacteria are listed as a potential cause of impairment. Combined sanitary and storm sewers around the City of Peoria might contribute to elevated bacteria concentrations during overflow events. The U.S. Geological Survey, in cooperation with the Tri-County Regional Planning Commission, investigated fecal-indicator bacteria (FIB) concentrations in this reach of the Illinois River and many of the tributary waterways during water year 2008 (October 2007–September 2008). Information regarding both diffuse- and point-source contributions of FIB will aid in any possible future resource-management efforts of these water resources at the Federal, State, or local level.

Hydrologic conditions during the study period are characterized as wetter than normal, with the mean annual flow in the Illinois River about 37-percent above the long-term average. Rainfall was normal to slightly below normal during the first three months of the study period; however, the observed rainfall across the State of Illinois for 2008 was the second wettest since 1895. Precipitation-recording stations within the study area had similar results as did the aggregated State-level records.

Two synoptic sampling efforts were conducted to determine FIB concentrations during low- and high-flow conditions in the waterways of the study area. The low-flow period was characterized during October 2007 sampling, and the high-flow period was characterized during June 2008 sampling. The Illinois River and 12 tributaries were sampled at 30 different locations during October 2007. The Illinois River and 5 tributaries were sampled at 17 different locations during June 2008. The Illinois River also was sampled routinely during the study period at the upstream and downstream boundaries of the study area, at Hennepin and Peoria, Ill., respectively. Additionally, fixed-interval samples were collected from three tributaries where streamflow was continuously monitored.

Concentrations of the two measured FIB—fecal coliform and *Escherichia coli*—demonstrated a statistically significant correlation to each other for all samples (r = 0.94, p <0.001), regardless of the specific sampling location. Correlation of FIB concentrations to streamflow also was investigated. A weaker statistical relation was found for streamflow to concentrations at any location. For the Illinois River water samples from the Hennepin, Ill., location or from any of the tributaries, positive correlation coefficients indicate that both streamflow and FIB values increase and decrease simultaneously in magnitude. At the downstream study boundary for the Illinois River below Peoria Lake at Peoria, Ill., however, a statistically significant negative correlation coefficient indicates a weaker inverse relation between values of streamflow and FIB.

Possible linkage may be evident between combined storm- and sanitary-sewer overflows with assumed elevated fecal coliform concentrations, based on previous investigative research by the City of Peoria, Ill., and measured concentrations in the Illinois River during June 2008. The data presented in this report indicate both diffuse and point sources of fecal indicators in the water column throughout the study area. The presence of one of the studied FIB typically indicates the presence of the other.

# Acknowledgments

The authors wish to thank USGS personnel who assisted with the intensive data-collection efforts required for this study: Jon Angel; Ryan Beaulin; Erin Bertke; Charles Bohall; David Fazio; Teresa Halfar; Marvin Harris; Robert Holmes, Jr.; Patrick Miller; Elizabeth Murphy; and Josiah Peoples.

# References Cited

Anderson, K.L., Whitlock, J.E., and Harwood, V.J., 2005, Persistence and differential survival of fecal indicator bacteria in subtropical waters and sediments: Applied and Environmental Microbiology, v. 71, no. 6, p. 3041–3048.

Cabelli, V.J., Dufour, A.P., McCabe, L.J., and Levin, M.A., 1982, Swimming-associated gastroenteritis and water quality: American Journal of Epidemiology, v. 115, no. 4, p. 606–616.

City of Peoria, 2010, Clean River—Healthy Riverfront Program, accessed August 2010, at *http://www.peoriacso.org/*.

Fry, J., Xian, G., Jin, S., Dewitz, J., Homer, C., Yang, L., Barnes, C., Herold, N., and Wickham, J., 2011, Completion of the 2006 National Land Cover Database for the Conterminous United States: Photogrammetric Engineering & Remote Sensing, v. 77, no. 9, p. 858–864.

Greenfield, R.E., 1924, Comparison of chemical and bacteriological examinations made on the Illinois River during a season of low and a season of high water—1923–24: Urbana, Ill., State of Illinois Department of Registration and Education, Division of the State Water Survey, Bulletin 20, p. 9–33.

Helsel, D.R., and Hirsch, R.M., 1992, Studies in Environmental Science—Statistical Methods in Water Resources: Amsterdam, The Netherlands, Elsevier Science Ltd., v. 49, 522 p.

Hoskins, J.K., Ruchhoft, C.C., and Williams, L.G., 1927, A study of the pollution and natural purification of the Illinois River—I—Surveys and laboratory studies: Washington, D.C., U.S. Public Health Service, Public Health Bulletin 171, 198 p.

Illinois Environmental Protection Agency, 2008, Illinois integrated water quality report and section 303(d) list—2008: Illinois Environmental Protection Agency, Bureau of Water 08-016, IEPA/BOW/08-016, 180 p.

Illinois State Water Survey, 2010, Climate events in Illinois archive, accessed August 2010, at *http://www.isws.illinois.edu/atmos/statecli/index.htm*.

Leadbetter, E.R., 1997, Prokaryotic diversity—Form, ecophysiology, and habitat, in Manual of environmental microbiology, Hurst, C.J., Knudsen, G.R., McInerney, M.J., Stetzenback, L.D., and Walter, M.V., eds.: Washington, D.C., American Society for Microbiology, 894 p.

Lin, S.D., and Beuscher, D.B., 1994, Indicator bacterial quality in the Illinois River at Peoria, Illinois, 1976–1986: Champaign, Ill., Illinois State Water Survey Research Report 126, 48 p.

Lin, S.D., and Evans, R.L., 1980, Coliforms and fecal streptococcus in the Illinois River at Peoria, 1971–1976: Urbana, Ill., Illinois State Water Survey Report of Investigation 93, 32 p.

Myers, D.N., Stoeckel, D.M., Bushon, R.N., Francy, D.S., and Brady, A.M.G., 2007, Fecal indicator bacteria: U.S. Geological Survey Techniques of Water-Resources Investigations, book 9, chap. A7, section 7.1 (ver. 2.0), available from *http://pubs.water.usgs.gov/twri9A/*.

National Oceanic and Atmospheric Administration–National Climatic Data Center, Annual climatological summary 2007 and 2008, accessed August 2010, at *http://cdo.ncdc.noaa.gov/ancsum/ACS*.

Sercu, Bram, Van De Werfhorst, L.C., Murray, Jill, and Holden, P.A., 2009, Storm drains are sources of human fecal pollution during dry weather in three urban southern California watersheds: Environmental Science & Technology, v. 43, no. 2, p. 293–298.

Statham, J.A., and McMeekin, T.A., 1994, Survival of faecal bacteria in Antarctic coastal waters: Antarctic Science Ltd., v. 6, no. 3, p. 333–338.

Wade, T.J., Calderon, R.L., Sams, Elizabeth, Beach, Michael, Brenner, K.P., Williams, A.H., and Dufour, A.P., 2006, Rapidly measured indicators of recreational water quality are predictive of swimming-associated gastrointestinal illness: Environmental Health Perspectives, v. 114, p. 24–28.

U.S. Food and Drug Administration, 1998, Enumeration of *Escherichia coli* and the coliform bacteria, in Bacteriological analytical manual (8th ed.), Rev. A, chap. 4 (updated 2002), accessed June 2011, at *http://www.fda.gov/Food/ScienceResearch/LaboratoryMethods/BacteriologicalAnalyticalManualBAM/default.htm*.

U.S. Geological Survey, variously dated, National field manual for the collection of water-quality data: U.S. Geological Survey Techniques of Water-Resources Investigations, book 9, chaps. A1–A9, available online at *http://pubs.water.usgs.gov/twri9A*.